Sh!t, Now What?

BECOMING A NEW ADULT

Sh!t, Now What?

BECOMING A NEW ADULT

E. Veal

3 DEGREES
publishing

Dedicated to my dad

contents

foreword

If anyone were to ask me who I am I would probably describe myself as a Black female engineer. My go-to response is to state my occupational status. Of course, I'm more than that. I am a daughter, sister, auntie, friend, volunteer, business owner, author, and more. However, if I have a job, I will daily be reminded that I am a Black female engineer.

For the longest time, I was just a Black female. I was raised in an environment where I was surrounded by other Black people. In my world, I woke up to Black people all around me, either caring for me, leading me, teaching me, serving me in stores, in churches, and in banks. I was surrounded by Blackness.

My neighborhoods were riddled with crime. I recall, at the tender age of six, begging my aunt to let me walk to the local grocery store with my cousins, who were about nine or ten. We all lived in the same neighborhood, so I was familiar with the route to this store; it passed by my house. I sweetly waved at my house and said, "Hi house!" as we walked by. In the store, we picked up whatever contents my aunt wanted. As we walked back by the house, I lifted my hand to wave goodbye (to complete the encounter) when I noticed a large fist-sized hole in the front door. I told my cousins who then told me to run as fast as I could back to my aunt's house. It wasn't until later, after overhearing a conversation, I learned that we'd been robbed. I promptly put my $2.67 in my purse and hid it under my mattress. My bed was just a mattress that sat on a metal frame.[1]   That's the moment I realized tragedy would soon be commonplace in my life.

I was in college when I learned that attending funerals wasn't common. By the time I was a senior in college I'd attended at least seven funerals. A few were great-grandparents and grandparents, but I've lost several family members to gun violence and bad health. Historically, and stereotypically, "Black" causes of death.

For most of my adolescence, I lived on or below the poverty line. I was not a stranger to low-income housing, welfare, or shared resources. Hand-me-downs and thrift stores were how we'd acquired clothes, shoes, or furniture. Sharing a room with my older brother was a necessity more than a desire. I can only imagine what trepidation my parents felt when I reached an age where sharing a room no longer made sense.

Growing up, it was routine for all the grandkids to hang out at grandma's house. Waking up and going to bed there was normal. We often left for school from her house. One thing we learned quickly was at grandma's house wasting resources wasn't allowed. I cringe as I recall

---

[1] Now that I think about it, if you just looked under the bed or slightly shifted the mattress, you would have found my treasure.

sharing bath water with my brother and two cousins.[2] Children naturally are anti-bathing, but when my grandma asked who wanted to take a bath first after a day of playing outside in the dirt, I piped up. When it was discovered I wanted to take a bath first to avoid "used" bathwater, I was forced to go second or even last. I would be faced with a bathtub filled with three inches of cold water where there was a solid mass of grime and dirt from three other children taking up at least an inch of space. It left a ring around the tub. I mastered the art of cleaning and refilling a tub with hot water without an aunt bursting through the door asking why the water was running. I truly believe it is due to these memories that I will not take a bath. The thought of sitting in my own filth repulses me.

This was my world. My Black world. This world gave me compassion, joy, and a strong willingness, amongst other things. At a young age, I was made aware that my Blackness was not enough and that I had to use what I was empowered with to be better. It was instilled in me that this world, my Black world, wasn't the "real" world. I was told that I needed to move mountains with my mind.

My dad retired as a painter. He painted ships and statues. Big shit. I still think it's cool that this was his profession. I remember we went to an event at his job and they brought out a statue.[3] And the foreman announced that my dad made it. (At the time, I wasn't paying attention and I thought that's what they said. In hindsight, I'm pretty sure they said he painted it.) I started jumping up and down with excitement. My dad

---

[2] Yes, you read correctly, bath...water!

[3] I want to say it was a man on a horse???

made a horse! It's super cool that my dad could point to something and say, "I did that."

Nonetheless, he would constantly tell me, "Erica, you're smart. You've got to do well in school 'cause, believe me, you don't want to use your hands to live. Use your mind." As a seven-year-old, I thought this meant we had the ability of telekinesis and my dad didn't use his superpower so he lost the ability and this was his way of telling me to practice.[4] Of course, it wasn't until later I realized he was talking about getting a career where they hired me for my knowledge and not the physical work I can do.

In the eighties, gender roles in the household were still enforced. Boys played outdoors while the girls stayed in the house. I have countless memories where all the females piled in my grandma's kitchen to cook Sunday dinner. I can still remember my mom teaching me how to light the stove with a burning piece of paper. We mashed potatoes and made spaghetti sauce from scratch.

While I very vividly remember these events, I also remember fucking hating it! The kitchen was hot, and I had no interest in knowing how to make tuna salad. I wasn't interested in wearing dresses or knowing how to sew a button onto a shirt. Makeup was never an interest. The most I wanted to do was paint my nails.

---

[4] I had (and still have) a very wild imagination!

In my teens, I'm sure my mother was annoyed with me constantly objecting and questioning any concept that put me in a gender-related box. I remember begging my mom to let me go cut grass on the weekends like my brother. While he was able to make spending money, I was forced to sit in the house and learn how to crochet.[5] I was fed up with being in the kitchen. One day I snapped and very matter-of-factly told my mother, "I don't want to do this because I'm going to make enough money to hire someone to do these things for me." My mother just stared at me, then told me I could leave the kitchen. She never required me to help her cook again.[6]

In school I found myself enrolled in courses that were dominated by boys. In middle school, I didn't notice right away I was the only girl in my shop class. It must have been after the third time my teacher "insisted" he "help" me. I recall measuring and sketching out all of my assignments, but I don't recall putting hands on actual wood (that's what she said).

In high school, I enrolled in Mechanical Drawing, only to have my teacher "help" me with my sketches. The "help" he provided always earned an A. This makes sense since my assignments were done completely in his handwriting! This proved to be very frustrating not only as a woman, but as a student that strived to earn top marks on her own.

---

[5] Which I must admit has come in handy much more than I expected #queenOfTheCrochetBraid

[6] Again, something I regret not knowing because cooking is just a basic life lesson! I'm a fucking idiot.

As a youth, I was stunted in my ability to grow in areas that were commonly male governed. Experiences like these were just the beginning of a string of events that made me acutely aware that I, a Black female, had limiting factors. That I would be underestimated.

Even with these experiences, going into the "real" world, I wasn't properly prepared for what life would hand me. I had no clue what I didn't know.

"You don't know what you don't know."

There are a lot of things I've experienced in life that my parents warned me about. They tried to impart wisdom upon me since they did have twenty-plus more years on this earth than me. However, as a young, dumb kid, I thought I knew everything. (Typical, kid!) There are also things in life that I've experienced that my parents have no experience with themselves and there was no way for them to give me insight. There are things that I had to learn either through trial and error, intensive research, or pure luck.

That's where this book comes in. There are things that I wish I knew before I was in that situation. Like taxes or the pros and cons of college. Even if you don't use all this information or understand it, having just a glimmer of understanding will help you navigate life just that much easier.

I hope you enjoy this book. If not, don't tell anybody. Just sucker them into buying it and say, "You should read it and tell me what you think." Thanks... 'preciate you!

sh!t lessons

You have this book because someone[7] thought you needed guidance on becoming an adult. Maybe you just ended high school and want to know what to do now. Maybe you just got out of college and you want to know what the "real world" has to offer. Maybe you fucked up somewhere along the way, and now you want to know where you went wrong. Maybe you know you are prone to fuck up, so you are trying to preempt the fuck-uppery. Whichever way led you here, one thing is clear: you don't know how to do this adult thing. You wish someone would just tell you what to do. But let's be real, you probably wouldn't listen anyway.

Let's be even more real, you probably aren't going to read this whole book. I mean...why? You aren't in school anymore, why the fuck

---

[7] Maybe, you.

you need to read a book? I mean, there are more than...**checks the last page**...more than a hundred pages in this book. What in the actual fat baby's ankle!? Why is this book so long? What can this book possibly be about?!

I authored this book hoping to be that voice I wish I had. The advice and guidance in these pages will give you a jumpstart on adulting. Don't misunderstand. I had great guidance with the resources that I had. However, I think I would have gone further faster, if I had a portion of some of the information I'm offering you.

You will learn (if you haven't already) that life is a journey. The trip is different for everyone. I'm sure you've heard similar phrases before.[8] When I first heard these statements, I really didn't know what they meant. I figured it was just a cliché that was a part of a cliché statement power pack that you unlocked at age thirty. The reality is that after years of adulting you start to analyze a lot of things. You wake up to what's going on.

The first and most disappointing thing you learn is your parents were right. Every obscure nugget of wisdom they gave you is going to come back to haunt you. Next, you realize that no one knows what they are doing. No, really! Absolutely no one knows what they are doing. Everyone is just either pretending, shadowing someone else, or surviving through trial and error. There isn't a step-by-step guide on how to do

---

[8] They are in damn near every self-help book.

these things. You can learn from the mistakes and successes of those that have come before you or you can fall and get back up and try again.

Nothing is guaranteed but death. I can promise you this, though, you will fuck up royally if you don't listen to *any* advice. You only know a fraction of what you *think* you know. It's best to start your journey thinking you do not have all the answers. Even if you think you do, listening to another person's perspective can open you to possibilities and opportunities that you haven't considered. The value in that is priceless. You may not need that information today, but it may hit you years from now.

My hope is that you actually read this whole book.[9] I hope that you will give it a fair chance to improve your life. Even if you don't read the whole thing, I wrote this book in such a way you can just pick and choose what sections you want to read. Clearly, I think that all the sections are good. I envision you'll eventually read this entire book all and think, "Damn, she was right. Her talent knows no end. My heart's desire is to be more like her and these brilliant words she's written." Nah. What I truly hope you think after reading the book is that you learned something. I hope to answer some of those questions that you had but didn't know how or whom to ask.

Let the journey begin!

---

[9] It's pretty damn good.

1

college

If your next step is college or you are considering college, this section is for you. Let me give you the bottom-line up front:

You are paying to do everything you decide to do in college.

I don't mean that in the figurative sense. I mean that in the literal sense. You are giving a community college or university actual currency to do whatever you have elected to do. Whether you go to college to study or party, it doesn't matter, you are paying for it. Do you want to break your dorm room door by playing human bowling? Probably shouldn't, but you could, and you are paying for it. Do you want to go to all your professor's office hours? (Something I actually did.) Go ahead because you are paying for it!

Your tuition money pays for nearly everything you do in college. Since college is typically too expensive for most people to pay for out of pocket. Generally, people take out student loans, which you aren't required to pay until four years later when you are done with school.

Out of sight, out of mind.

This strategy enables you to think of paying for college as an intangible situation, making it extremely easy for you to blow away your college opportunity. Without the constant reminder that you are paying for these educational services, you tend to forget that you are your own enemy.

If your tuition is overpaid, then you'll probably get a refund check. Refund checks are issued if you have a grant or scholarship that covers a larger portion of your financial charges than expected by the student loan. This is not a gift. Those refund checks aren't free funds. Its money back from your loan. The loan that you must repay. Additionally, bank and credit unions charge a percentage rate to borrow the money; this is called interest. As a result, not only do you have to pay all this money back, but you also have to pay the interest on it! Receiving a refund check is the financial equivalent of "a moment on the lips, a lifetime on the hips."

Unless you are attending school on a scholarship, take very seriously what university you attend. Deciding between in state or out of state, community college or university, ivy league or a historically Black colleges and universities (HBCU), the school you choose will come with a price tag.

Most graduates are proud of the school that they attended. You see bumper stickers and baseball caps stamped with the school they'd chosen. I've worked with people that have graduated from Harvard to Lindsey Wilson College. I used to be intimidated by individuals who had a degree from a "well-known" college or university. I thought that somehow, they were better than me since they were from *FancyPants University*. Then one day someone pointed out, "Yeah, but you both have the same job." Sometimes, we look past the obvious. It took that one statement to change my whole perspective on my background. Although we had different college journeys, we still managed to have the same outcome and by my calculations, I am not in as much debt as that individual who paid for a "name brand" university. I offer you this: take the smarter route of less debt. If you must get a degree from a "name brand" university, consider taking as many classes at your local community college, and then transferring to the university for graduation.[10]

Don't feel slighted if you can't get into that top-shelf university. Going to a "normal" school doesn't automatically imply you know less. In many cases, because they want to make sure you are prepared for your next phase, state schools often over prepare you. I have a friend that went to Duke University for medical school after attending a local state university. She told me that the local university's Organic Chemistry course allowed her to shine over her peers!

---

[10] Not all credits are transferable so double check which courses can be transferred first.

Somehow, we got into our minds that what school we went to would forever affect our careers. Oftentimes, we feel that we aren't able to get a job due to the name of the school we attended. I'm here to tell you that no one cares! Employers care about what you know, not where you went to school. I've been in and conducted many interviews, and not once has the name of the institution been a factor. Most employers care more about the experience you've had.

When I was in graduate school, I made the foolish mistake of taking out a $18,000 student loan. I needed to pay rent. My graduate stipend was dispensed in large lump sums, and I hadn't received my check for the semester. In hindsight, I should have asked for help, but I thought I was on my own and I had to figure it out. After not paying rent for two months, the property manager started leaving 'Where's my money?' notes on my door.[11] That's when I decided to take out a student loan to supplement my housing while in school.

By the time I started paying off the loan my total had skyrocketed to $21,000! *So, you're telling me in two years your loan increased $2,000!?* Well, it wasn't done in two years. It was actually done over the course of about six years. *Six?! Where did six come from!?*

Of course, after I graduated, I didn't have any extra money, let alone any money to pay off a student loan regardless of the payment. Yet, they still wanted their money. I reached out to the student loan agency

---

[11] Another lesson to learn is: Dem bills gotta be paid! Landlords and property managers don't care that your school was late paying you. You need to pay them. But I digress.

once I got out of college to see what they could do to assist. That's when I learned there was something called forbearance. Little did I know, forbearance is the devil! Basically, forbearance allows you to not pay on your loan (yippee!) but it continues to add interest (boo!). You can request a forbearance for up to twelve months at a time for as long as you want. However, your loan provider will eventually want their money, so you won't be able to push it off for that long. You've done nothing but push it off for a while. For your loan provider, they will likely grant you a forbearance for a while since it's no impact on them. They will get their money. For you that means that your loan will be even higher when you start to pay it off.

What I should have done is asked for a **deferment**. With a deferment, depending on your loan, the government pays the interest on your loan while you get your shit together. Obviously, it's harder to get a deferment. You must meet certain qualifications to get one, such as unemployment, extreme economic hardship, enrolling in school at least half of the time or active military duty. It's definitely worth attempting at the very least.

What I'm noticing is this section is called College, yet you are just talking about finance and loans and other math-related stuff. Why, Sway?!

I want you to know information before it's too late to make better decisions. They expect people fresh out of high school to already know about loans and interest rates, yet it's not taught in school. There isn't even an afterschool program for it. It's absurd that banks allow fresh adults (newly eighteen-year-olds) to take out multiple loans more than

$10,000 a semester. I mean, think about it. You are literally reading a book about how to be a damn adult and you think that you are equipped to make financial decisions in the thousands of dollars price range. The likelihood that you've ever contemplated that you are making thousand-dollar decisions probably never even occurred to you until right now! Shit! I'm still paying off that $18,000 loan today![12]

My goal here is to scare you into understanding that college is something that will affect you financially for a large part of your life. You'll either pay for it now or pay for it later. Choose to spend your money wisely. Everything counts. If you take a class and fail, you still have to pay for it. If you skip your eight a.m. class every morning, you still have to pay for it. If you sign up for a meal plan but eat out every night, you still must pay for it. There aren't any real refunds when it comes to school. If you spend two years taking Basket Weaving, then decide you want to change your major to Astrophysics, you are welcome to do so. But guess what? You have to pay for it. As you embark on this journey, keep your financial future in mind. Every decision afterward will depend on it.

Now that I've scared the bejeezus out of you about the financial part, let's get into the fun stuff!

Before I continue, I'd like to give you a bit of background on who I was when I entered undergraduate. I was seventeen years old when I started college. I'd finished high school with *magna cum laude*. I'd taken every math class I could take in high school. I was awarded the Dozoretz

---

[12] I just logged in my account and as of April 2020, I have $3100 left to pay. I've been out of school for 14 years! Let that sink in.

National Institute for Minorities in Applied Sciences (DNIMAS) Scholarship.[13] At the time, this was a full four-year academic scholarship at Norfolk State University. The scholarship paid for everything! Room, board, books, tuition, and fees! Literally any financial barrier that could have gotten in my way, the scholarship took care of. All I was required to do was keep a 3.8 grade point average (GPA) on a 4.0 scale for the entirety of my college career in a science field i.e. Math, Biology, Chemistry, Computer Science, Engineering, or Physics. I also couldn't get more than one C in the four years I was in school.

Since I'd grown up poor, this was literally the only way I could go to school. My mother offered to pay my way to any school I wanted, but she was a single mother of three and taking on a four-year tuition was insane! Although tempted by the offer (because I wanted to go to a school away from home), I "settled" for the local state university. To the locals, the state university was the natural next step to schooling. Basically, going to this university meant you were just going to thirteenth grade. All in all, I had one shot at higher education, and it was at Norfolk State University in the DNIMAS program.

Right about now you are probably thinking, "*Did she just give me a whole dissertation on financial aid and student loans and this broad had a full free fucking ride?!*" Yes. Yes, I did.

---

[13] Now called the Dozoretz National Institute for Mathematics and Applied Sciences.

While I can't personally relate to student loans during undergraduate, I can relate to another looming number that dictated whether I go to school or not. My GPA. Every semester I had to make sure my GPA didn't slip. Maintaining a 3.8 GPA in a science field is hard. In addition to that stress, I constantly reminded myself that this was my only shot at a college education. My family couldn't afford to send me to school and I, sure as hell, didn't have the money to send myself.

I recall many people stressing to me that your freshman year is an important year. Specifically, the first semester of your freshman year, but what they don't tell you is *why* your freshman year is the most crucial. First and foremost, your freshman year determines your GPA. The higher you can get your GPA your first year, the better off you will be throughout your college career. Unfortunately, people don't make this realization until it's too late.

The number of credit hours and your grade in that class determines your GPA. It can get a bit complicated. You can skip this part if you want but the math nerd in me *needs* to explain this mathematically.

nerd • math

Every course that you take has a certain number of credit hours associated with it. Typically, these credit hours equate to how many hours you will spend in class per week. Two credit hours are typically a Monday/Wednesday class or Tuesday/Thursday. Three credit hour classes can be Mondays/Wednesdays/Fridays or maybe a three-hour lecture on Thursdays.

Say this is your grading scale below:

Grade	Weight
A	4.0
B	3.0
C	2.0
D	1.0
F	0.0

To calculate your GPA, you follow this equation:

$$\frac{(\ Credit\ Hrs\ \times\ Weight) + (\ Credit\ Hrs\ \times\ Weight) + ...}{Total\ number\ of\ credits}$$

If your first semester you take two three-credit hour classes and earn an A in both, no math is needed to know that you have a 4.0 GPA.

Sem. 1	Grade	Wt.	Credits x Weight	Total
3 cr. hrs.	A	4.0	$3cr.\ hrs \times 4.0$	12
3 cr. hrs.	A	4.0	$3cr.\ hrs \times 4.0$	12
			$\dfrac{(\ 12+12)}{(\ 3+3)} = \left(\dfrac{24}{6}\right) = 4.0$	

Let's say the next semester you take two three-credit hour classes, but you received an A and B.

$$\frac{(4.0 \times 3cr) + (4.0 \times 3) + (4.0 \times 3) + (3.0 \times 3)}{12}$$

$$\frac{45}{12} = 3.75$$

Your GPA just went from a 4.0 to a 3.75! No amount of A's will get you a 4.0 ever again. Mathematically, it's not possible! That's why you need to get the highest GPA and take the highest number of credit hour classes in your first semester. You want to start off with the best possible GPA. As you can see, maintaining a high GPA is pretty difficult.

Dude, you said 'Let's get to the fun part,' then you started talking about GPAs and doing math. I don't know about this book. You're starting to bum me out.

Oh! My bad! Maybe we have different definitions of what 'fun' is, says the math nerd.

On to the actual good stuff. If you are fortunate enough to live on campus, you will experience what I like to call adult limbo. You are technically an adult and can pretty much do whatever you want. If you are fortunate enough to either live on campus or with your parents, you don't have to worry about living expenses.[14] Generally, you don't have any real bills. Just a nice purgatory between high school and the real world. This grants you freedoms that you didn't have before. You can easily succumb to peer pressure. When you don't have to answer to anyone, and you can

---

[14] I recognize that not everyone who goes to college or even newly adulted is without responsibility. While some of the information will pertain to you, I only have the aspect of a new adult without major responsibilities.

hang out after midnight and don't have someone breathing down your neck reminding you to do your homework, you start to see how it's easy to forget important things like your GPA and how you are paying for everything you do.

A lot of universities have restrictions on some things that freshmen can do. At my university, freshmen living on campus couldn't have a vehicle on campus nor could they join a sorority or fraternity. My scholarship program restricted us from participating in campus clubs and activities. These were all put in place to encourage freshmen to do better their first year. This typically isn't explained. You just find out later that they were just looking out for your (and their) best interest: your tuition check! Yet as a new adult, it's easy to rebel against these rules to prove you are an adult and you "don't need anyone telling you what to do," when in reality, you do. You have been coddled in high school, and the university knows you are ready to go ape shit! Only one in three freshmen return for a second year. Think about it: would you pay thousands of dollars to do something that you failed at once before? When put that way can be difficult to say you would. Attrition is an important aspect for universities. It's in their best interest to have *your* best interest in mind. If you do well, then you are more likely to stay and continue. If you stay, they continue to get paid. Failing can spark your memory that you are paying for this experience. I honestly think "I'm paying for this" should be your motto while you are in school.

I'm not going to sugarcoat it. College is hard. It's a level of hard you have never experienced before. There is an infamous saying: "If you want something you never had, you must do something you've never done." This surely is applicable when it comes to college. That saying and our previously stated motto should be the two driving motivational phrases that get you through college. They will also help you overcome any anxiety over where you should ask your professors for help to succeed during your college years. Remember that you get out what you put in. If you aren't clear about something your professor mentions, I highly recommend you ask them questions until you understand.

I mentioned earlier that I went to all of my professor's office hours. This is a 100 percent true story. It was my junior year. By this time, I switched my major from Chemistry to Applied Mathematics. The scholarship program required us to participate in a summer session, pre-college courses to prepare us for the real thing. It was in the summer session where I learned that I was a fucking idiot. Not really, but sort of. While in high school, I'd gotten used to being the cream of the crop, one of the smartest students in the school. In high school, classes weren't challenging, and I could breeze through them without even trying. Yet here I was, in a pre-college physics course with students from different parts of the U.S., and I quickly learned that I was trash. Like USDA-certified trash. In NSU's DNIMAS summer session, I learned what it felt to feel challenged. It is also where I fell in love with the teaching style of my Calculus professor, Dr. Jawed.[15] I vowed to take all of his classes. He was the first professor that explained the "why" in math. I'll never forget

---

[15] Name changed.

that it was him who told me what the hell is the point of an integral. There was an extra flourish to his handwriting whenever irate he became at our idiocy. I admired this dude. (I still do!)

I still recall how I asked on the first day of Differential Equations if we could use calculators in the class. I received glances that suggested I was a fool for asking such a basic and rhetorical question. Although others thought it an odd question, I'd taken enough of his classes to know this was a necessary question. We all watched as he pondered, "To be safe... no." Record scratch. No? Wait, we are in Differential Equations. That sounds hard as hell. How will I calculate my calculations without a calculator? These were the rumblings throughout the class. For me, though, I just laughed.[16] I tell you this to give you context to what I'd faced in my third year at university.

As the semester approached midterms, it also approached the drop date. The drop date is the absolute last day you can drop a class without it ruining your GPA.[17] As I approached midterms, my grade in Differential Equations approached a D. For those that don't remember, I was on a full scholarship that had very strict requirements to stay in the program. Let's recall the terms of my scholarship:

- Must maintain at least a 3.8 GPA at all times
- Can't earn more than 1 final grade lower than a 'C'

---

[16] Thanks, Dad, for the calculator. I literally never used it.

[17] Remember, in college, the two things you always are trying to protect are your GPA and your money.

Differential Equations was a four-credit course. A 'D' calculated into my GPA as a 1.0. Therefore, my GPA and my scholarship would suffer gravely, if I failed. I was at a crossroads. Looking at this you're probably thinking, *Crossroads? Duh, drop the class. I see how you got that D now.* But the idea of dropping out of a math class as a math major was idiotic to me. Why am I a math major if I can't pass a math class? Dr. Jawed paid special attention to the math majors in the class. He scrutinized our work more harshly than the other students. He would state, "You are a math major! You should know better," as he deducted a point for missing a negative sign. While some may have called this singling out, it did make me a better mathematician. I valued his opinion and didn't want to let him down. I consulted him before I made my decision. He told me, "You have a chance at passing this class. But you have to do every problem in the book." Some people may have brushed this off as if it were just a passing phrase that means "work harder." However, I knew Dr. Jawed literally meant, "Do every problem." With that, I decided to stay in the class.

Yes, he was dead serious about doing every problem in the book and[18] yes, I did just that. My math major friend, Grace, and I decided we both were going to do every problem. We monopolized his office hours. I recall once, he saw us approaching and preemptively stopped us, saying, "Girls, I can't today. I need to grade papers." I think that's when we both realized that we had been hogging his time. We'd become so focused on conquering the class that we ignored everything else. Our drive to succeed

---

[18] Well each section we cover, which was damn near the whole book.

in the class, not only required that we make sacrifices, but also utilized our resources.

The day had come for the final exam. I don't remember too much about that day. I think there were about ten questions on the exam. He sat in a chair holding the door open. For some reason, I had a calculator. I think maybe he said sure when someone asked if we could have a calculator for the exam. The exam was cumulative, meaning it included everything that we'd learned since day one. I had taken a deep breath and flipped over the exam.

Question one. Hmm...it was easy. I thought, *maybe he wanted to give us a freebie. Yea, right, the man who said 'no' to using calculators in a Level 300 math class.*

Question two. Hmmm...equally easy. I'd glanced around the room; everyone was buried in their paper. Some people were click-clacking away on their calculators. I didn't even turn mine on, so I don't know what they were calculating. I'd finished the entire exam in twenty minutes. I'd glanced around the room again. It seemed that I was the only one done. I went over my work. It looked right. I went over it again. Ten minutes had passed. The university's policy allows each student two hours to complete an exam. I was confident that I'd done my best work. I got up with my exam in hand. I felt everyone's eyes on me as I stood and handed my exam to Dr. Jawed. He looked at me, then asked, "Already?" At that moment, I panicked a little, but I assured myself that I'd done all I could do to pass the class. I gave a strained smile and replied, "I guess."

He nodded and wished me a good holiday, and with that I left for the winter break.

Before the end of the year, I found out my final grade. I had gotten an A! What the what?! The exam grade was an A and my final grade was an A. I was confused. I immediately thought there was a mistake. When classes were back in session, I went to his office and asked him if he remembered my exam score. He smiled and he said, "Of course! You had the highest exam score I've ever given." What!? My eyes bulged out of my head. I replied with, "Whaaat?! Noo. I mean... I feel like you gave us those questions before. Were they homework questions?" He said they weren't, and that they were questions from the end of each section. He admitted he had some issues selecting the questions since he knew that my friend and I requested his assistance on some of them, which meant he couldn't assign those particular ones. I walked out of his office elated and proud that I managed to put my all into something and it worked out in my favor!

I told that whole story not to just brag about how I totally kicked Differential Equations in the ass, but also to describe the level of difficulty college can get. My Differential Equations professor wouldn't let us use calculators. Let that sink in. Imagine taking a course without a calculator where one of the formulas looks like this:

$$V = \frac{1}{a} \sum_{n=0}^{\infty} P_n(\cos \theta) \left(\frac{r}{a}\right)^n$$

Next, imagine what I needed to sacrifice in order to solve every problem in every section and attend all the office hours of a professor.

Each section had maybe forty problems and some had parts A-G. Oh, did I mention that I had no less than twenty credit hours each semester? Twenty credit hours is borderline insanity considering a fulltime student typically only needs about twelve credit hours. Recall: a credit hour is the number of hours you spend in class. Not only did I spend twenty hours in the classroom, but I had to study for each of these classes. College was starting to become a forty-hour work week. This sounds lame, but this is what you signed up for. This is what you are paying for.

I don't want to mislead you into thinking that I was a study bug, and I didn't do anything but calculate how to increase my GPA. I had a full college experience. I went to parties, participated in pranks, snuck in dorms, and pledged in a sorority. To illustrate how back and forth college can go, let me take you into my senior year. As a young lad, I watched an amazing show called *A Different World.*[19] *A Different World* is an American sitcom based on the student life at a historically black university. The show addressed several topics that related to the college experience such as racial and social injustices. This show inspired me to join a sisterhood of college educated women, also called a sorority.[20] I also learned that the process to join a sorority can not only take a toll on you physically, but also on your GPA.[21] Therefore, early in my college career, I'd decided that I would pledge later in my tenure at the university. I knew I would be too

---

[19] If you haven't seen it stop reading right now and go watch all six seasons of it. I'll wait.

[20] A sorority is a sisterhood and a fraternity is a brotherhood.

[21] GPA is BAE!

excited to graduate to focus on actual course work, so I planned out my in order "bird" courses my last semester.[22]

When my last semester was arrived, it was my time to pledge. The call had gone out for the sorority I had my eye on. I'd put my name on the list (metaphorically speaking). There was only one issue. I didn't have all bird courses my last semester! Yes, I'd planned it out perfectly, but what I didn't take into consideration was the fact that a class is automatically cancelled if fewer than eight people signed up for it. This caused a major issue for the three graduating mathematics majors: Grace, Cora, and me. We'd all pretty much been in all the same classes for the last four years. All the math professors knew us by name. This perk came in handy when we had to advocate for three of our required classes to be offered the final semester so that we could walk across the stage. Otherwise, we'd have to wait two years for the next graduating class of math majors!

Advanced Applied Mathematics, Numerical Analysis, and Real Analysis were the three classes we needed in order to graduate. They didn't even sound like they were easy classes! Nevertheless, I was determined to pledge my last semester. I had a dream, dammit!

Each of those classes were three credit hours. Two of the classes they managed to get some engineering and physics students to take the course, which enabled us to have over eight students. Real Analysis ended up being a class we had in our professor's office three days a week.

---

[22] Easy classes like Intro to Bowling. Come on you haven't seen Sister Act 2. Again, stop and go watch it. I'll wait.

Pledging a sorority means late nights and early mornings. You must still maintain your class schedule as well as study for them. Yet, in addition to that you must also fulfill your duties as a pledge. Those duties may require you to wake up late at night or early in the morning to get them accomplished. Being a pledge varies from sorority to sorority and fraternity to fraternity. I remember attempting to study for my midterm in Advanced Applied Mathematics at the same time I was pledging. It was a take-home exam where the professor allowed us to work together. To a novice that may sound like a butter exam, but to us seasoned academicians that just meant just the opposite. We had a week to turn it in. Every night for a week we all gathered around a chalkboard in the library. Our method was to divide and conquer; we'd split the exam so that a couple of people worked on one problem. It took two people all week to come up with a solution for one problem! I would go to the sessions that *started* at midnight and attempt to be a valuable member to the group. However, around my sophomore year I'd taught myself that it's better to just go to sleep and wake up early to study than to attempt to stay awake. At a certain point my mind doesn't retain any of the information. I can read an entire page of content and couldn't tell you what the last word I read. I can admit now that I was not a valuable member of that group exam. It was not my proudest moment.

Oftentimes, I would either forget to do an assignment or forget what day it was and miss class. Alas, Grace and Cora were my clutch! They knew pledging was something I wanted to do, and they kept me in line. They helped me remember to turn in assignments and stayed up late with me to study. After weeks of hustling, I finally concluded my initiation into the sorority. My GPA suffered like I anticipated. It actually suffered more than I anticipated. I'd earned a C in my African American History class. Previously, I'd earned a D in Physics my freshman year, putting me on academic probation. Recall: if I received another C or below, I would lose my scholarship. For six semesters, I was on pins and needles hoping that I didn't fail any class. But alas, I'd earned a C in African American History. Let me tell you a feeling you never want to feel: being the first in your family to walk across a university stage, but to get a call a month later stating that you received a 'C' in African American History and you need to repeat the course to get your degree. Yes, you got it. I got Dikembe Mutombo'd at the finish line (or whatever...sports.) I was appalled at the audacity of them thinking I was going to go back to take a class. *I am a graduate. How dare you, sir?*

Joining a sorority or fraternity is just one of the ways that you can gain the college experience. The beauty of college is that it offers a large range of activities and groups that will allow you to bond with likeminded individuals. You can participate in sports, the band, and an assortment of clubs. The things that you learn in college aren't always educational nor are they always apparent until later in life. Some of the tokens I managed to take away with me are:

- Time Management: Being able to juggle classes, relationships, and parties isn't the easiest thing
- Public Speaking: When I used to speak in public it always sounded as if I was about to cry. I didn't have a desire to cry, but you

wouldn't have been able to tell that from the way my voice quivered when I read a presentation.

- Small hints in the corner of my presentation: To give you an indication of what's on the next slide, add a word that will remind you what's coming up next. Make sure the font is like 6-point because you don't want it to distract your audience.

- Speaking in the plural: When you give presentations, you speak as if everyone participated even though you *know* everyone didn't. Say, "After thorough research, we found that the mitochondria are the powerhouse of the cell." Instead of, "After I tried to track down the rest of my group and they were nowhere to be found, I, me, a whole me, found out that the mitochondria are the powerhouse of the cell. Apparently, I'm the fucking mitochondria of this group."

2

not college

There is no need to go to college simply because your family expects you to. If you know that you aren't about that college life, skip it. You can still succeed. And I don't mean that sad-ass success whenever they say, "*You can live a fulfilling life without a degree,*" but they really mean, "*We need managers at Sunglass Hut.*" When I say succeed, I mean you can still make just as much money as those who went to college.

One of my favorite stories to illustrate this is about a college professor I had. Let's call her Dr. Watkins. One day, she invited a handful of students, me included, to her house for dinner. I mean broke college students rarely turn down free food. When we arrived, we all zeroed in on the giant trampoline she had in the backyard. (Apparently, it came with the house.) After jumping our little hearts away, we gathered around the deck for some grilled food made by her husband, Mr. Watkins. Mr. Watkins was an automotive mechanic. That'd been his trade for years and he had perfected his profession.

Dr. Watkins was a very open and welcoming professor who shared many personal details with us. One of the tidbits that she shared was that their household was "old fashioned." Mr. Watkins insisted on paying all the household bills. He told her that the money she earned was hers to do as she pleased instead of contributing to the home. As a college professor, she made a significant amount more than her husband; however, his salary afforded them a beautiful (dare I say) mansion with two luxury cars and other amenities that gave them a very comfortable life. It was at this point that I'd realized I'd have a preconceived notion about mechanics. I thought that people of the working class were destined for a life of lower class. Growing up that is what I'd seen and as a child couldn't fathom anything greater. It was in that conversation, I was awakened to the idea that everyone with a vehicle needs maintenance, albeit a tire rotation or body work. A mechanic will forever be needed if we have vehicles. Even electric vehicles need a mechanic (tires aren't immune to maintenance). Therefore, a mechanic's expertise is not only needed, but will always be sustainable. We need mechanics not just for cars, but home appliances, farm equipment, sewer devices and much more. Just imagine if we had to purchase a new thing every time it broke because we didn't have mechanics. The world would be on fire! Also, imagine this for a second. You're in charge of a private school. You find out that there is a knocking sound coming from your school bus. You are now in a position to hire a mechanic to fix this bus. Consider the type of mechanic you'd hire. Would you hire the cheapest person? Hey, why not? Let's save some money. Now ponder why he may be so cheap. Maybe he is starting a new business and needs to build up new clientele or get high ratings on Yelp. Or...maybe he is straight trash! Maybe he cuts corners or uses the cheapest materials. Would you let that individual maintain your school bus that transports someone else's kids? I'm not trying to imply that just because something is expensive it automatically means that it's quality, but I'm saying someone that is worth their weight will charge you their worth.

The longer I'm in my career the easier it is for me to advocate for those that don't want to or can't go to college. I literally can't remember how often I've used the actual information that I learned in school. Don't get me wrong. I am thankful that I went to college. I can guarantee you that I wouldn't be where I am if I hadn't gone to Norfolk State University. But I have learned that a formal college education doesn't mean shit. A common misconception—let's been honest—a common stupid idea from college-educated people is in order to have success you must be knee-deep in college debt. Smart and rich is typically synonymous with college educated. You've heard that a lot of very famously rich people are rich and smart. No need for me to rattle off names. You know them.

By no means am I discounting your ability to achieve that type of success if you don't go to college. However, a lot of the aforementioned individuals are outliers, or people that significantly differ from the statistical normal. Ugh, I was hoping not to mention them, but I want to prove a point. Take for instance Mark Zuckerberg or Bill Gates. These dudes dropped out of college because they were confident in a product that they were creating while in school. They are entrepreneurs. Entrepreneurship doesn't require a degree. If you invent something that changes the world, no one cares if you went to school or not.

You can go online to find a plethora of career opportunities which don't require a college degree. Commercial pilot, pharmacy technician, air-traffic controller, and damn near every IT position, are just a few of the positions that don't sound basic as hell. Typically, people who say you can still make a living without a degree typically mean positions that require a lot of physical labor.

While many of these positions don't require a degree, they usually require some type of licensure or certification. The job I currently have, I need *zero* degrees for. Every employer I've had looks for a list of my certifications. Everyone I work with is completely blown away when I tell them I have three degrees and two of them are master's degrees![23]

Acquiring a certification requires you to master the specialty you are studying for. For example, if you want to become an Amazon Web Services (AWS) Solutions Architect, you would study for the AWS Solutions Architect exam. Duh! I did a month of intensive studying for the exam. I took an in-person, one-week course, watched videos online, and read whitepapers. Fortunately, a lot of my costs were reimbursed by my company; however, it could have cost me about $2500. Yeah. That's a lot of money. But when you compare it to $80,000 for college, it's a rather small price to pay to potentially have a six-figure career.

However, I want you to know that getting a certification isn't cheap. The exam itself can be $150 to $1500. Some certifications require

---

[23] Not sure if I should be offended or ...

you to take multiple exams. The Microsoft certifications that I have required me to take three different exams. Each one required the same level of effort. Still, that's only three months out of my life compared to the four years for college.

If you are fortunate enough to already be employed, check if your employer will reimburse you for training. Please take note of two important parts of the previous statement. First, the word training. A lot of companies have allocated funds for their employees to get educated in areas that directly pertain to their position, and that will increase the marketing value of the company. You can't just get training in anything. If you work for a construction company, you can't necessarily ask for training in IT security if you don't plan to transition to that position. From a business perspective, why would they train you for you to leave the company? However, if you are in construction but ask to go to Project Management training, that is something that can be useful inside and outside the company. There is a certification attached to it as well. A Project Management Professional (PMP) is a noteworthy certification.

The next word to pay attention to is reimburse. It means that you are paying for the course upfront. This is pretty standard. Employers want you to understand the situation. They want you to understand this is serious. Typically, they have you sign an agreement that states you will be reimbursed if you pass the course. This gives you more incentive to pass. Albeit, more pressure too, but incentive, nonetheless.

Certifications and licensures can take you far and they target what you are interested in. Not going to college isn't the end all, be all. Success, in whatever fashion you prescribe, can be yours.

3

friends, how many of us have them?

There are two similar metaphors that I like to think of when it comes to friendship. The first says, "People enter our lives for a reason, season or lifetime." I believe I was well into college when I first heard this statement. It helped me in more ways than I expected. It helped me to cope with loss, friends, and significant others. When someone exits my life, I try to find that reason they were in it.

The second metaphor is from, interesting enough, Tyler Perry's character Madea. I'm not the biggest fan of Tyler Perry films.[24] Before I discovered I wasn't a fan, I watched a few of his films and plays. When I'm moved by something, I don't care where it comes from. The impact still

---

[24] I just searched Wikipedia to see what he has created to see if I could caveat this statement but not. I'm not a fan.

takes hold. I'm not sure which film or play this came from, but I think it's one of the most insightful comments about people.

Madea:

"I put everybody that comes into my life in the category of a tree. Some people are like leaves on a tree. The wind blows — they're over here. They're unstable. It blows the other way — now they're over here. The season changes. They wither and die. They're gone. It's alright. Some people, most people in the world are like that. They're just there to take from the tree. They ain't there to do nothing but take and give shade every now and then. That's all they can do. But don't get mad if people are like that. That's who they are. That's what they were put on this earth to be what they are, a leaf.

Some people are like a branch on that tree. You've got to be careful about them branches too cause they'll fool you. They'll make you think they're a good friend and they're real strong, but the minute you step out there on them they'll break and leave you high and dry.

But if you find two or three people in your life that are like the roots at the bottom of that tree, you are blessed. Because they're the kind of people that ain't going nowhere. They ain't worried about being seen. Don't nobody have to know what they're doing for you but if those roots weren't there that tree couldn't live. You understand? A tree could have a hundred million branches, but only a few roots down at the bottom to make sure it gets everything it needs. I'm telling you, when you get you some roots hold on to them, but the rest of 'em, let 'em go. Just let it go. Let folks go."

When adulting, you find that friends and friendships play more of a role than you ever suspected before. Right about now you are beginning to realize that you *don't* know everything and that you *can't* do this on your own. You are going to need a support system more than you'll ever allow yourself to admit.

Before we begin, let me break the news to you now: the friends you have, you probably have because you were in school with them. *What? No. Wait. What?!* Yep.[25]

While in school you developed your closest and longest relationships. Think about it. Most of your time is spend in school or after-school activities. There's an external entity that facilitates bonding. Any venturing out to find new friends happened with a controlled situation. This simple fact is one that takes a lot of people a long time to realize. At some point you are going to ask yourself, *"How did I make friends before? I made friends all the time."* Now you have your answer.

In this chapter, I want to introduce some insight on friendship that are tough to swallow. I didn't know these things upfront, so it wasn't easy for me. Hopefully, you will be a little less taken aback by the notions when you are presented with them. Maybe you'll even think back to this very paragraph.

---

[25] Now obviously this statement is geared towards those who were privileged enough to have a full school experience. Yes, it's a very generalized statement.

you • will • lose • some • friends

Nah, not me. I made friends easily. I'm just going to skip this section because she's not talking about me. Ahem. Playa. I'm *definitely* talking about you. This is by far the hardest of the lessons to learn. No one wants to lose friends. No one thinks they will, but we do.

Going back to the metaphors at the beginning of the chapter, people come into our lives for reasons, seasons, or lifetime. Losing friends just means they were in your life for that season. Don't negate what you had just because they aren't around any longer.

One reason why we lose friends is because what we define as friendship is constantly changing. We learn what we desire in a friend and what we don't want in a friend. We start to see how our definition of friendship. These are the *leaves* Madea mentioned. For that moment in your life they were needed, but after that moment passes you let them go.

Another reason we lose friends is lack of communication. Some people we hold in high regard yet the direction of our lives lead, pull us away from each other. In the beginning you will fight for the friendship, but eventually it will die and that's ok. That friendship, while seasonal, was also for a reason. It taught you something. At bare minimum, it taught you how to cope with lost love. Maybe not in the traditional sense, but it taught you how to move on knowing that someone significant shared a moment in time with you, and that separating was the natural order of things.

The final reason we lose friends is fallout. Someone said or did something that could not be overlooked, or your relationship wasn't mature enough to cope with the situation. Sometimes you realize in those moments that maybe you both had different ideas of friendship. I've fallen out with many friends. From learning that I was being talked about behind my back to feeling disrespected, I've lost one friend after another. I'd love to put most of the blame on the other party, but I know I've had my fair share of missteps in ending a relationship.

I very vividly recall losing one of my best friends via instant messenger. When I was in my freshman year of college (this was back in the Netscape, AOL, and LimeWire[26] days), I had recently been told by a guy that despised me that my "best friend" was talking to our "nemesis" about me behind my back.[27] When I confronted her, she revealed that she'd always had an issue with me being close friends with her boyfriend. This annoyed me because her boyfriend and I were friends before they'd even met! I was annoyed that she expected me to terminate a friendship simply because of her dating life. Ladies and gentlemen listen up. This high school mentality needs to end! Expecting your significant other to not have friends of the opposite sex is insane. They had friends before you

---

[26] I'm pretty sure you are going to have to Google some of those terms

[27] Yes, I thought it was strange that he'd told me this and to this day, I still don't know why he did. However, I'm forever thankful.

and asking them to stop associating with those friends can be considered selfish and insecure. Anyway, back to my issue. I let her know that I thought it was asinine that she expected me to terminate my friendship. I assured her that I was *not* going to stop being his friend unless he requested so, and that if she couldn't handle it, then that would be the end of our friendship. Of course, I didn't say it as eloquently as I just did. That was the gist of the message. Let's just say we haven't really spoken since and I'm ok with that. It may have hurt in the beginning to know that I was losing someone that I thought was my best friend, but in the end, it was for the best. Her and I didn't work out as friends, but I am still friends with that guy to this day.

making • friends • takes • work

When you were in school, all the people were right there. If there was a new kid in town, you simply had to go to school to meet them. You made no extra effort to find a friend. If they didn't go to your school or were in your scout league, you probably didn't go out of your way to get to know them. You barely knew any kids that went to another school. Making friends was unequivocally easy when you were in school. Outside of school, there isn't an institution where there is potential to make friends, and suddenly you're at a loss.

So, where do you get friends? The solution: you now must make a conscious effort to leave the house to seek out people. As a twenty-something, going out isn't hard to do at all. You damn near go out every night.

Now you are out in the streets, at the club, and you meet a group of folks. You take shots with them. You all get pumped because your jam just came on. You exchange numbers since the tequila has kicked in and made you besties for life. Now what? Are you calling these people the next day for brunch? The next time you want to go to the club, are you giving them a call? Do you think they are going to follow up with you about that trip to Tijuana? You and I know that's a great big "Hell No!" You probably will delete the number within a week or two. You go out again next weekend with the same intention and it ends the same way.

It's going to take you your entire twenties to realize that you spent so much time with your friends because you were in school together. You are going to constantly wonder why your friends were around for so many significant moments. It's solely because they were always around. As an adult, you don't get that luxury. You must try to reach out to those people that are important to you. You must put in real effort to enjoy time with them.

There is no formula for making new friends. If you move away from your hometown or your friends move away from you, finding new people that you trust will take a real amount of effort. If you are alone, you may need to seek out local groups and clubs. Playing a recreational sport or participating in a social club are some ways that you can find new people to hang out with. Luckily, this is the age of technology and finding people in your area that are interested in similar activities as you have become easier than ever. You can download an app like, Meetup, to simply filter for a new kickball league or Dungeons & Dragons group.

Social media can aid in keeping up with your old and new friends. With its invention, you can now keep up with the minute details of each other's lives. Our friends can know just about anything about us, at any time. Our outfit. Our lunch. Our haircut. There is so much social interaction that there barely is any reason to connect with each other.

When we do connect, we don't have to spend a lot of time catching each other up on what it is that we did last Tuesday. We'd just open Instagram and boom! there it is.

Group messaging apps help me to connect to my true friends. As your life events starts to fill your time, it's harder to update people individually. Group apps let you post, "Kim's pregnant!" You get five or six "Congratulations!" A few minutes of counting the number of kids in your social group, then that's it. Until someone remembers someone's birthday. The same thing happens. Rinse and repeat. It seems very impersonal, but it keeps you connected. My groups are people I care deeply about. They are the people I want to know my dog died or my dad has cancer. I want them to know the un-Instagramable details of my life.

Friendship sometimes means making a conscious effort to let people know how things are going in your life, even if they don't ask. That's difficult to do since naturally, we don't want to put a damper on anyone's day. However, if you need help or support, you can't always rely on your friends reaching out to you; you need to let them know. One thing that I've started to do with my friends is when they ask, "How are you?" I tell them the truth. I'll say, "I've been sad lately," "I'm fantastic!" or "Stressing over this new job, but it's great!" Going with the automatic, "Fine and you?" doesn't give your friends true insight into how you are. You need intentionally strive to let folks know.

---

every • friend • isn't • universal

One afternoon, I was with two girlfriends, Brianna and Amelia, at a bar for a drink. We'd somehow started discussing travel plans for the summer and Brianna mentioned that she was going to Montreal with another group of friends. Jokingly, Amelia and I feigned offense because we hadn't gone on a trip together. Brianna nonchalantly proclaimed, "Well, y'all aren't universal." Her statement offended me, but I said nothing for fear of ruining our time. Amelia, on the other hand, was more forthcoming with her disapproval. Brianna described how she felt that her other group of friends were more open to doing different things and were more flexible. They were universal.

This conversation offers an inside look on how I learned that friends aren't universal. It made me think about what things I was willing to do. We all like to think that we are universal, but we aren't, and we shouldn't be. Everything isn't for everybody. Look back at your own friend groups. You have several. Church friends. Work friends. Neighborhood friends. And that's just fine. Friend groups become the norm as an adult. After realizing that you must work to make friends, you then realize that you can't just hang out with those friends on any occasion. One of the best examples of this is traveling. If you are fortunate enough to travel with your friends, you will learn more than you anticipated. Traveling with anyone, friends, or family, will give you an inside look into who they really are. The first time I went on a trip with some friends, I realized quickly that we shouldn't travel together. When I go out of town, I like to hit up restaurants that are staple to that locale. When it came down to dinner time they wanted to go to McDonald's. Now, I'm fully aware that in other countries they offer things at McDonald's that aren't offered in the U.S. However, when we are in Seattle, I refuse to go to McDonald's.[28] When I'm in New Orleans, I want to hit up Cafe Du Monde, not Dunkin' Donuts. I like to call the people that like to go to chain restaurants when they are in a new area Chicken Finger People. These are the people that will ask for chicken fingers at any restaurant.

I have a group of five women that I travel with yearly. We all like to try new things and pretty down for whatever. We are all the same level of bourgeois. We have been to Mexico, St. Thomas, and Abu Dhabi just to name a few places. I find that I rarely see these women outside of these trips. We barely even speak to each other. However, when one of us has an idea to go somewhere, the other five of us are down for the ride. No question. This is an example of how friends may not be universal but have their specific purposes.

---

[28] If you *really* know me, you know I straight up refuse to go to McDonald's in general.

Brianna and I recently went on our first trip together. We backpacked through Europe for two weeks! She is one of my root friends, someone that holds me up. We recognized that this two-week trip was either going to make or break us. With this in both our minds, we set out on our trip. In the beginning, we were insanely considerate of each other. Further into the two weeks, we realized we enjoyed doing similar things and were able to relax. She was nervous that I was going to be very structured. I had already decided that this was a spiritual journey for me and had no intention of it being structured. It all worked out and she and I learned that we each had a new person that we could travel with.

While she is one of my root friends, it doesn't necessarily mean that she is universal. I have a solid group of friends that she's never met because they serve a different purpose for me. Additionally, having a space that is yours is very healthy.

Needing to have a group of friends that you spend all your time with is unrealistic. Everyone isn't into everything you are. You will not have any cool stories if everyone shared your same experiences. Keeping separate circles of friends is normal and necessary.

4

dots and circles

Mentors are like God's way of saying, "Hey! Here is someone with the wisdom of a real adult but the chill factor of your homie." I love mentors, and for as long as I can remember I've always had one. My mentors may not have been the same person throughout the years, but there was always someone that I can pinpoint as a mentor throughout my journey.

What is a mentor, exactly? Well, good ol' Webster Dictionary (aka Google) says that it's "an experienced and trusted adviser." I mean ... yeah but ... it's a little more to it than that. I mean if you wanted to simplify it ...yea you could say that, but I mean... umm...That actually sums it up perfectly. It is a trusted someone that has had several experiences more than you.

The key word in Webster's definition is "trusted." It is up to you to determine whether you trust this person's decisions. This is not to say that someone isn't trustworthy. On the contrary, someone could be the most trusted confidant you know, but if you don't trust their decisions then they probably shouldn't be your mentor.

Huh? What? What do you mean that you trust them but not their decisions? Take this situation: Your best friend is a good, honest person. They live life as one big adventure, taking odd jobs here and there to keep themselves afloat. You joke around and call them a rolling stone because they are always on the move. Would you trust this person to give you advice about the best places for a vacation? Totally! They've been everywhere, they know all the great places. However, you probably wouldn't go to them about how you should diversify your 401(k).[29] Sure, they can give you their opinion on the topic. However, it's quite unlikely that they have implemented any of the information that they give to you.

Now that we've defined what a mentor is, let's talk about how to go about getting one. I believe a true mentor/mentee relationship grows by pure coincidence (hush up, folks that don't believe in cowinky-dinks). Good mentors develop from a common bond, and along the way you recognize the mentorship. Most people that you choose as your mentor are chosen subconsciously. You find yourself wanting to know what they think about important issues: What school should I attend? Am I ready for a dog? Should I pay my rent or get these Yeezys?

The perfect mentor/mentee relationship is kind of like an old, cheesy rom-com movie where your eyes meet from across the room. I find

---

[29] More on 401k in 401k

it very rare that you find a great mentor by formally introducing yourself and requesting that they be your mentor. I've had someone approach me this way before, and it felt very much like an interview. It was very odd for me to be their mentor, although I was very honored. It felt forced and unnatural, and very different from the freeform relationships I was used to. This relationship didn't last long. Most mentor/mentee relationships that start like this tend to be for a specific reason known upfront. Once the individual reaches their goal, the relationship fizzles away.

Not all "forced" mentor/mentee relationships fizzle away. When I went to college, the scholarship program I was in paired each freshman with an upperclassman. This was to help give us insight on how to navigate the program. I still communicate with people from that program, as well as my mentors and mentees. This relationship allowed freshmen to have a confidant in the program which otherwise would probably not have occurred. This same concept is adopted in some companies. New hires are paired with someone in the same discipline to have a go-to person where they feel safe and free to ask "stupid" questions.

While this approach can spawn a rewarding relationship, my best mentor/mentee relationships have grown organically and blossomed fruitfully. Well, as organically as me going to a sorority meeting and my soon-to-be mentor sitting across from me can be. Whether you pledge Delta Delta Delta or Delta Sigma Theta, sororities are loaded with women who love to pass down their wisdom.[30] Social groups are another great place to find mentors. Where else can you find like-minded people with a wealth of experience and can't shut up about it? I found mine in a sisterhood.

The person that you make your mentor is typically someone you admire. You can admire their marriage, the way they organize their life, their makeup game, or how they manage school, work, or a business. Mentors are versatile and wonderful people. But not everyone can do it all, which leads me to another point. You don't have to have just one mentor. You can have a mentor for every facet of your life. (Although, that can get cumbersome.)

A mentor doesn't necessarily have to have the same experiences as you in order for them to give you solid advice. They just need to have had more experience. More experience doesn't necessarily equate to an older person. Everyone goes through things at different points in life. Therefore, a mentor can very well be someone that is younger or even the same age as you.

While they may not have gone through these things before, they know who you are as a person and can give an objective opinion. This is important because you know that the information given to you is out of love without you feeling as if they are being vindictive or spiteful. Mentors genuinely have your best interest at heart and want to see you succeed.

---

[30] Case and Point: I wrote a whole book!

They share their wisdom with you, leaving you to make positive decisions for yourself.

Currently, I have three sets of mentors: financial, career, and personal growth. Yes, sets. Meaning more than one mentor. Multiple people allow for more diversity of information as well as increased availability. If I'm struggling over whether I should get faux lashes and my one person is busy, then I might just end up with lashes that make me look like Mr. Snuffleupagus. With a myriad of mentors, you can get many different opinions and concoct your own conclusion. But I wholeheartedly believe you should start off with one person: your dot.

My friend and I came up with the term dot when she realized that she didn't have a person to bounce her brilliant ideas off. She was getting bogged down with 5011[31] things and there was no one that helped her put things in perspective. I explained to her that she needed a circle of trusted advisors to help her. Not realizing how overwhelmed she really was, she panicked at the suggestion that we bring more people into the clusterfuckery that was happening in her world. That's when I suggested baby steps: just get one person...start with a dot. I volunteered to be her dot and she could make a straight-line connection to me (I'm a math nerd, I know). This helped her.

Your dot is essentially your primary mentor. This person serves as one whom you trust their advice the most. They have a great number

---

[31] Read as "fiddy-lemen"

of life experiences. Your dot almost always gives you the best advice. They are level-headed and force you to view the situation from a different perspective.

Over time, you get comfortable with your dot and expand your circle of mentors. Everyone in your circle will have their place. The advice that you get from one mentor may not be the same type of advice that you get from another.

Diversify your circle. It's always good to have mentors that look like you as well as some that don't look like you. Young, old, male, binary, white, Asian, Christian, Jewish, Republican, Libertarian, you name it. Mentors from different backgrounds give you a different perspective.

Take note as to where and how your mentors get their information. Don't be afraid to ask questions. If they are your mentor, then they will be willing to share this their sources with you. The mentor/mentee relationship should be an open and honest relationship. Just remember that not every mentor is an expert in every aspect of life. That's why I have three different sets of mentors.

Not every person that you admire is fit to be a mentor. Through time you'll find that even your great heroes have flaws. I have mentors that have excellent career advice but make terrible financial decisions. However, I do listen to their "could've, should've, would've's". These are the things they could have done or should have done or would have done if they'd know what they know now. This could be the best advice; their hindsight is now your foresight. Use that information. Make wiser decisions. I believe the best example of this is retirement plans. I have heard many seasoned employed individuals speak about how they wished they'd started saving for retirement when they first started working. The older minority generation didn't have the privilege of retirement plans because they had to make ends meet. They probably didn't start saving until their late forties (if at all). Some individuals were fortunate enough to have a company that gave out pensions, but these days there are only a handful of companies that offer pensions.

To date, my dot has been my mentor sixteen years. She initiated my circle. She has given me advice, support, and free food. Sometimes all three at the same damn time! Her home has become my second home and my family knows her family. She has become the big sister I've always wanted. Someone that I can openly talk to about finance, love, and a host of other things without feeling judged or berated. She is probably closer to my mother's age than mine, but I don't feel the age difference when we hang out. If you asked her, she'd say that, I've given her as much as she's given me. From this side of the fence, I couldn't pay her back even if I tried.

As time goes on, you'll start to see that more people come to you for advice. Most of the time, you just give advice, unknowingly realizing that the mentee has become the mentor. I first recognized I was a mentor when I had a younger co-worker ask me about homeownership. For me, I was just giving him information off the experiences I'd had. Yet, he'd seek me out for more and more advice. I was becoming a mentor without knowing it. I was taken aback when I started to think about the people along the way would ask Should I rent or buy? Why should I go to community college first? What's the point of college? How do I set up a 401(k)? To me, these questions were not hard to answer, but they made me a little more conscious of the advice I gave. I had to start making sure that the advice I gave had context and fit with their goals. Eventually, you will become someone's dot. Although, you think you are ill-prepared to mentor someone, you hold more knowledge than you'd admit.

So, the lesson from this chapter: Get a mentor. Become a mentor.

5

even beyoncé
took a year off

Women tend to look out for everyone but ourselves. We have somehow been programmed to think to put others first. We neglect self-care. This has to end!

Take a note from every airline instruction guide ever:

Please place the mask on yourself first, and then assist your child or other passengers.

This information is given because in order to help others, you must first help yourself. If you can't breathe, how long do you suppose you are going to be able to assist others? Here is a hint: not very long! This can be thought of as a metaphor for self-care. If you aren't taking care of yourself, how long do you think you are going to be able to keep assisting others? Need a hint?

I have a friend who is notoriously known for being a badass chic! She is an Ivy League graduate with a law degree. Kicking butt and taking names is her mantra. In 2013, when she became pregnant, she didn't bat an eye. She continued to kick butt and take names until...she confessed to me that she was exhausted. I couldn't empathize with my friend. Since I'm slightly older than her, I'm typically able to offer up advice. I sat there on the phone lost for words, when suddenly the only words of wisdom I could muster up to share were,

"Even Beyoncé took a year off!"

For those that don't recall, when Beyoncé revealed she was pregnant with Blue Ivy, she'd already been incognito for several months. This was quite unusual since Yonce is known for how hard she works to put on a flawless show. Although the world was just catching Blue Ivy Fever, Bey had long been missing in action. Whether it was doctor prescribed or her own rule, Beyoncé was no longer on the scene. She later revealed that she had to put herself first to be the best mother for her daughter.

The advice I offered my friend was simple: you don't have to "do it all." If Yonce didn't, why would we?

---

h a v i n g • i t • a l l

For some strange reason, we think that we must have it all. Not only should we "have it all," but we should have it all right now.

Take Beyoncé, a prime example of someone who "has it all" in the public's eye. She had to take a year off because her craft was so demanding—sixteen hours a day when preparing for a performance—and it was hurting her home life with her daughter. And that shows that having it all really either means you *don't* have it all or you are stressed and overworked. It truly is an illusion.

The notion of "having it all" also puts into people's minds that they have to have it the moment they're out of school, and that they shouldn't have any struggles. Well, news flash: you're going to struggle. When we look at megastars like Beyoncé, all we see is the final result— her wealth, fame, beauty, etc. People see that and think, "Oh, I can do that!" and then after twenty minutes they expect to have it all. For most of us, it doesn't work that way. Every normal person goes through struggle years. These years usually have a lot of instant ramen and a strong focus on gas money and transportation. This is the journey. No one likes this journey because it's rough and hard, but it happens anyway. Don't delude yourself into thinking you *have* to have it all, or that your friends who seem so content with their lives have it all together.

I remember the moment I realized that "having it all" was an illusion. I was still in graduate school, but it was coming to an end, so I was also teaching at a public high school. I drove a '99 Honda Civic.[32] I

---

[32] Let's be honest, I would probably still own to this day if it hadn't got totaled.

lived in a crappy apartment in a building across the street from my graduate school. I stayed there because the rent was cheap.

Looking back, it truly was a shit show. Once, the air conditioner was out and the temperature had to be a cool 110° in my upstairs two-bedroom apartment.[33] I recall smelling marijuana from my downstairs neighbor as if he were sitting right next to me.

To continue painting this picture of the neighborhood, one day I was awakened at four a.m. by the sound of my marijuana-smoking neighbor's disheveled girlfriend crying hysterically in the hall. She had one breast hanging out of her shirt and mascara running down her face. Shit. Show.

Now, let's meet my friend, Amelia. She was also a teacher at a local public high school. However, she'd just closed on a two-bedroom condo in a recently developed neighborhood and had an Acura TL-whateverthefuck. I constantly berated myself for not having a portion of what she had. I couldn't figure out what she was doing that I wasn't. I needed to get out of that hell hole!

One day when she came over, I finally mustered up the courage to ask her how she was able to do it. How can she possibly "have it all" when I'm over here living the #struggleLife? That's when she said, "Oh

---

[33] In hindsight, I don't know why I had a two bedroom. Literally no need for it.

girl, my dad put the down payment on my house to get my payments to a price I could afford, and my car is leased."

My mouth dropped. I couldn't believe I'd been bamboozled. Here I was questioning every decision I made to figure out why I was losing in life and not #winning like her. Truth was, she was presenting an illusion that I fell for.[34] I've never been so grateful for a moment of clarity. That single moment launched a series of events that made me into who I am today.

After she told me that, I figured out how to get a house on a teacher's salary.[35] From that point on I figured if it seemed too good to be true, I needed to verify. I suggest you do the same. I promise you will run into more people that tell you it wasn't as easy as it seems.

So, when people romanticize my life now, I make sure they are fully aware of the journey that got me here. The heartbreaks, low credit scores, robberies, struggle meals, and the like. I like to be fully transparent about my journey because the truth is, I didn't have it all then, and I don't have it all now. Neither does Beyoncé or anyone else, so don't give up that precious time with your friends and family for the sake of an illusion.

---

[34] Disclaimer: She was not trying to bamboozle anyone. She was just afforded opportunities I wasn't.

[35] Which is totally shit! I thought about how I couldn't have kids unless they came out with a salary and 401(k)! The people that teach you how to fucking read should get all the dollars! Like how do you teach a muthafucker to read?! Bitch, I don't know! Ok. I'm done ranting.

be • selfish

I advocate for women to be a little selfish. I've had many tell me, "That's not really in my nature." What I hear is: "I feel bad being number one in my life." Stopping to recognize that you are just as important than all the other people and things on your list is the first step to self-care. Taking the time to pamper yourself can make a world of difference.

Pampering doesn't necessarily mean you need to go to Elizabeth Arden's Red Door and get the most expensive massage package. It simply means taking a few minutes of your day to recognize yourself. It could simply be five minutes in a quiet room meditating.

When I was working on my masters in Optical Engineering, there was a professor that wasn't too far from my age and she said to me, "Get a massage. It will change your life." Once she said it, I thought that was a strange statement. I could barely pay my rent, let alone afford a massage. In my mind, massages were hundreds of dollars, and only folks that are fully established in their careers could afford them. Nonetheless, I hadn't forgotten her words.

A few years later, I found that I was constantly rubbing my shoulders from being hunch over a computer for many hours of the day. I was starting to get overwhelmed with school and transitioning from the comfort of school to "real life." Since, I had a little money in my pocket, I decided to peruse the Internet to see how much it was for a massage. I discovered that my area had a local massage school that heavily discounted their rates so massage school students could practice. Score! I decided to go to the massage school to get me a thirty-five-dollar massage!

I learned from my discounted experience that she was absolutely right! It did change my life. It was after the massage that I realized I was living a life where I didn't take care of myself. I thought getting a massage was wasteful and selfish. I could spend my money on things that were more important and necessary. To me, getting a massage was synonymous to getting my nails done. I thought paying someone to do my nails was bonkers! I can do my nails at home.

But that massage though.

It allowed me to gain a new perception. It showed me how to relieve my stress. That massage was the first time I can remember doing something for myself and fully enjoying it. In order for me to get the most out of the massage, I had to relax. I had to allow someone else to be in control (something I was very reluctant to do). Once I calmed my mind and convinced myself that the world wouldn't catch on fire the hour I was in my massage, I was able to fully enjoy my experience. That one massage told me that it's ok to splurge on myself. It was ok to take time to make myself first.

From the massage, I started to do other things that allowed me to take an hour or two for myself. I now get my nails done.[36] Getting my nails done affords me the pleasure of having someone attend to my needs after tending to other's needs. Yes, I can do it myself, but why!? Now, I will take myself out on a date or have a me day. As Tom & Retta would say on *Parks and Recreation*, 'Treat yo'self!" It doesn't happen often, but enough to replenish me. Sometimes that 'Treat Yo'self' comes in the form of taking a nap in the middle of the day or vegging out on the couch and just watching movies all...day...long. I'll order all my meals from an app because I don't want to put on pants. Sometimes these days happen in the middle of a workweek, and I'll request sick leave for a mental health day. I understand not everyone is afforded these opportunities. Sometimes self-care is just sitting in your car for ten minutes before walking in the house or listening to relaxing music. I like to color. That's right, with crayons and a coloring book. They have adult coloring books, but a children's coloring book can work too! Regardless of how you can do it, take a break for yourself. It's important to your mental well-being.

w o r k o u t

Most of my life, I've been overweight. I can't recall a time when the scale ever said 115 lbs. For me, it felt like it went from 88 lbs. to 160

---

[36] Even though I know I can do them at home

lbs. No numbers were in between. Just a little kid weight to a fully grown adult.

By the time I went to college, I was a smooth 177 lbs. I left college at about 189 lbs. Then 2008 happened and I'd become the heaviest I've ever been: 240 pounds! I was constantly hearing from physicians that I was in the "overweight" category, and that my BMI was too high...blah blah blah. It was endless, reminders that I was fat, and that just made me want to eat more. I had a friend once say, "I'm fat because I eat, and I eat because I'm fat." While I know that he said this to spark a laugh from the group, it ended up being some of the truest words I've ever heard.

When I was younger, I was always jealous of skinny people. It seemed that life was just fairer to those that looked more like society's standards. I thought it was unfair that I needed to exercise while they just woke up like that.

In graduate school, I realized that I had to take care of me and sought how I could become healthier. Through some friends, I learned the YMCA allows people with low income to "suggest" a membership price for consideration. After some adjustments to the price, the YMCA gave me full membership to use the facilities. I decided to start going to the gym at six in the morning. I figured no one would be there to witness me attempting to lose weight. Boy, was I wrong! Apparently, six a.m. is that time when skinny people were working out![37]

---

[37] I do recognize there are people out there with strong metabolism and not all "skinny people" are necessarily healthy

The gym was FILLED with fit people! I was like "OOOOHHH! They do work out." They were working just as hard (actually, harder) than I was to stay fit and healthy. This information changed my entire outlook on working out. I was no longer jealous. I was calmed to know that these skinny people were just as concerned about their bodies as I. No longer did I feel like "the fat girl" in the room; I was just late to the game.

One of my major problems with working out is that I hate working out. My argument for not working out was that I'm an engineer and as an engineer, I try to find the most efficient way of doing things and working out totally negates all logic. It's literally moving when you don't have to. Running in a circle, pointless. Running on a treadmill, pointless. Picking heavy things up and putting them down, pointless. Squatting in an imaginary chair, silly and... pointless! I could not wrap my head around going to the gym. What was everyone's motivation? To me, it seems like everyone that works out enjoys working out. I grew tired of hearing comments like, "Ugh, I haven't been to the gym in two days, I feel horrible." [insert eye roll] or "I love running in the rain!" [insert disgust face and side eye] or "After a workout, I have so much energy!" [insert confused face] My inner dialogue was sounded more like, "Energy! What the fuck do you mean energy! I am devoid of energy. The only thing I want after a workout is to lie on the ground and not move!"

Whenever I heard these comments, I felt like there was something wrong with me. I didn't have that thing that made me like exercising. It was like watching everyone enjoy ice cream and having no idea what the fuss is about. It was as if I wasn't born with the "I love to exercise" gene.

Feeling different on top of looking different made it that much harder for me to get to the gym. I despise going to the gym (present tense). Gyms are boring. There is nothing to do but … work out...eww. Not only are they boring but you have to go with a plan! You have to prepare for the gym! Is it going to be leg day? Arms? How many reps should you do? How long should you run on the treadmill? My gawh! What is this, school!?

Since I wasn't properly educated on how to exercise, I would just run on the treadmill.[38] I would do that for about thirty minutes, build up a really good mist on my face, and that would be the entire workout. In my mind, cardio was how you burned the fat off. I feel like this is a normal routine for a lot of overweight females. From this point of view, it's quite understandable that unfit women grow tired of working out and quit very early on.

After years of trying to lose weight, I feel like I've read every blog and "Get Un-Fat Quick" guide out there. Lots of blogs suggest that weightlifting helps you lose weight instead of tons of cardio. I started weightlifting and I started to enjoy that. Why is that you ask? Weightlifting involves a lot of sitting! Just sit and lift shit. I was all about sitting down while exercising.

Quickly, that became a nuance for me since I had to have a plan on how I would balance upper and lower body workouts. Some people like

---

[38] Let's be real, walk...really fast...ok fast-ish

the opportunity to customize their workout plan, however, I felt I was putting way too much effort to put into working out. The more effort I had to put into it, the less I wanted to do it. Having to come up with a 30-60-minute workout was doing the M-O-S-T!

I tried exercise class after class in search of something that was a workout but didn't feel like a workout. You know how people lose weight after they start playing a sport? I wanted to have fun while working out. I tried Zumba. It's quite embarrassing being a Black woman with no rhythm trying to dance. Even if I managed to catch part of the beat, I'd start thinking, "Why is this called dancing? What makes this a dance?" Next thing you know, I've become confused and frustrated. That's when I'll stop and walk out of the class. I recognized that I'd spent a very large part of my finite life crafting excuses to keep myself right where I was instead of growing into who I was meant to be.

One day, whilst strolling through Groupon (like any single thirty-something year old), I found a Groupon for boxing classes. It was unlimited classes for a month for twenty dollars. It sounded like a great deal and I'm all about a good deal. I took a class and immediately fell in love. I liked that I wasn't focused on working out. I didn't feel like I was exercising. I was focused on getting the technique right and making sure my form was correct. By the end of the class, I had sweat dripping from places I didn't know could sweat.

It was the first time I'd ever signed up for a one-year membership to ANY gym at full price.[39] It actually took me a month to sign up because I was nervous that I wouldn't be able to last the entire year. I didn't think that I would stay passionate about it. I was worried that it was just a fleeting high and in three months, I wouldn't go back. I took a chance on myself and paid the near $1000 yearly fee. Since I'm cheap, I calculated that I needed to attend at least four times a month to get my money's worth. I was psyching myself out before I'd started, but once they had my money, I committed myself to four times a month (at a bare minimum).

Surprisingly, I found what I was looking for: a way to exercise without it feeling like exercise. I started to understand those eye-rolling comments. After being in a routine, stopping for two days interrupts the whole flow of things. I still hate working out. I hate going to the boxing club. I mentally have to prepare myself every time I go. However, once I get there, I enjoy learning new skills and feeling the adrenaline rush after the workout. In my mind, boxing is more like learning a self-defense skill than exercise.

Throughout my journey what I've learned is that you can **want** to do something all day long, but if you want to be serious about creating a better life for yourself, you must dig yourself out of your comfort zone and make it happen. Jen Sincero in *You Are A Badass at Making Money* says, "You can have your excuses, or you can have success. You can't have

---

[39] Well not full, I did catch a sale!

both." I find that this not only applies to making money, but also to any endeavor you are trying to overcome.

I love that I've decided to take care of me. To take an hour of every day to make myself better. Working out, albeit for weigh loss or just fitness, is a great way to show self-care. There are days when I don't want to work out (and I don't) but overall, I remember that I am doing this because in the end it makes me feel good to know that I am working towards a better, healthier me.

eat • right

Finding a workout regimen that I enjoy was extremely helpful in my weight loss journey, but what I learned is the most helpful is eating properly. You hear it all the time: "Weight loss is 20 percent in the gym and 80 percent in the kitchen." It's the most annoying statement when you've been struggling with weight loss (right up there with "I love running in the rain!") It's annoying to those who haven't experienced it. It also seems like the percentages should be switched around. Even so, I hate to be 'that guy,' but it's true. There are countless stories about how some folks can just cut soda from their diet and lose weight. There are so many things that we put in our mouths that we don't count when it comes to calories. Some examples are candy, gum, alcohol (and not just fruity...like a shot of vodka has like sixty calories alone!), juice, sauces, cereal, coffee, etc.

Eating right is about making better choices. A lot of the time we find ourselves making excuses as to why it's ok that we eat unhealthy for a particular meal. Such examples are I'm out with friends; I don't come to this restaurant often, so I should get my usual; I've never been to this restaurant, so I should try something staple to this establishment; I'm on vacation, or it's Friday.

Just like learning skinny people workout at the ass crack of dawn, I also learned that they eat like rabbits all the time. It's enlightening to discover those times that you see them out chomping down a triple-decker double cheeseburger. I know a guy who constantly posts Instagram pictures of the food he cooks on the weekends. BBQ, brisket, baby back ribs, Flamin' Hot Cheeto chicken wings, and bacon-wrapped mozzarella balls are just a few of the things he has posted. Instead of being a 550 lb. dude, he is a fit dad. I finally inquired how he is about to eat such lavish foods and stay so fit. He pointed out that he only eats those things on the weekend; during the week he eats a can of tuna and cottage cheese for lunch every day and runs six to eight miles every morning. He is willing to "suffer" through the week to get rewarded on the weekend.

Before, I assumed God loved skinny people more than me and wanted me to have a #struggleLife. But in reality, I was overlooking the work that was being put in to stay fit. They were working hard to live a healthier lifestyle, too After all was said and done, the ugly truth is I was living this life by choice.[40] It wasn't impossible to get fit. People were doing it every day.

They say all the time that if you want to lose weight, you have to change your lifestyle. Diets are dumb. If you try enough of them and waste enough money, you'll realize it too. Weight loss occurs when you change your thought process. Realizing and accepting that eating healthy is literally the #struggleLife. The key to weight loss is simple math:

$$intake\ calories\ <\ burn\ calories$$

Regardless of anything else, that is the simple fact. You must burn more calories than you take in. If you take in fewer calories, you don't have much to burn.

There are lots of factors that are against you when it comes to calorie intake or eating healthier; with the number one factor being: you just don't want to. Food is too damn good. You say that you're going to treat yourself this time. But "this time" falls on a Tuesday and you can't start eating right in the middle of the week. So, you tell yourself that you'll start first thing next week. This becomes a continuous ritual until you just say, "Fuck it, gonna eat what I want." About four months later, you start the process all over again. I get it. I don't want to have to eat like a rabbit during the week. My remedy was portion control. Portion control is something that very common amongst overweight Americans—especially

---

[40] #spoilerAlert duh!

students. It's very difficult to stop yourself from eating something that is good. Especially if you want more. They say stop when you are satisfied, not when you are full, or when your plate is clean. If I'm completely honest, sometimes when I'm full, I'm still not satisfied! I want to somehow engulf myself in the deliciousness of the meal. Learning portion control isn't easy. I learned a few tricks that helped me. Such as when I'm at a restaurant, I immediately ask for a box with my meal so I can put half in it to go.

At home, I stopped buying snacks for the house. I recognized that my laziness trumps my hunger. Currently, I live in a high-rise building. If I really want something, I would have to get dressed, go down fourteen floors to my car, drive to the grocery store, get out the car, go in the store, figure out what I want, purchase it, drive back home, go back up fourteen flights, and then enjoy it. That is way too much! I wanted to stop typing because there was too much happening! If I did all of those things, you better be damn skippy I wanted it.

Another thing I use at home is a meal delivery service. Since I live alone, their lowest plan, dinner for two, would last me two to three meals. For me, knowing that I didn't have to cook two to three meals was enough to continue portion control. Also, since I don't like going to the grocery store nor figuring out something healthy to cook, the meal delivery service was perfect. I initially hated it because I don't like cooking. However, I don't think I've spent more than forty-five minutes cooking a meal. After I cooked it, I would pack it up into one or two Tupperware bowls and put it away in the refrigerator. That way if I wanted something else, it would be cold by time I was done cleaning the kitchen. (I'm personally too lazy to reheat anything by that point.) As I said before, portion control isn't easy, but it allows you to keep forth progress on your weight loss journey without having to compromise taste.

There are many different ways to change your eating habits. It is best to go in thinking, "Can I do this for the rest of my life?" It sounds extreme, but if the answer is no, you need to find something else. Trying to convince yourself that you can eat tuna and cottage cheese five days a week is counterproductive. You will probably last a week and then go H.A.M.[41] on the weekend to the point where it negates all the suffering you endured during the week. Make sure you have a solid life plan.

---

[41] H.A.M.-Hard as a Motherfucker

6 be a feminist

I wasn't always a feminist. This was mostly because as a youth, my view of feminism was skewed as having to be "anti-feminine" in everyday life. I wrongly associated it with bra burning and no-shave-vember and thanks to the media, embracing feminism during that time was wildly unpopular. Thankfully, times have changed, and so has the definition and perception of feminism. Still, the concept isn't an easy topic to breach for many and can be even more confusing for young adults trying to find and shape who they are.

There have been countless times that I have had someone whisper, "Are you a feminist or something?" I would look at them with a perplexed look and say, "Yea. Aren't you?" Some people would feel pressured into saying, "Yea." Some would mumble their way out of the conversation. Those that would tell me yea, I'd ask, "What does feminism mean to you?" This question would surely stump them. Now, by no means am I the authority for the discussion, because I know my feminism is also flawed. I can't recite a clear definition of what it means to be a feminist.

Sometimes I have a hard time drawing the line between feminism and harmless jokes. The most popular (and in my option the most accurate) definition of feminism was made known by Chimamanda Ngozi Adichie (popularized by Beyoncé's song, "Flawless"):

A person who believes in the social, political, and economic equality of the sexes.

This simply means the rights that a man is afforded should also apply to a woman. Socially, if a man can go out without shaving or a shirt on, a woman should be able to do the same. Not that she will do the same, but she shouldn't be punished for making the same decision a man made. Socially, women are looked upon as differently than a man simply because we have an "innie" and they have an "outie." Other than that, we crave the same things in life. We all want food, fun, and friends. We want to be safe and have the ability to explore the world.

Politically, a woman should be able to rise to any level of an office. Technically, here in the U.S., she is able to do that. Historically, we've seen this isn't true. A very public example of this is Hillary Clinton. She has constantly been limited because she's a woman. I just googled her, and the first description was she was "Former First Lady." While this is true, it belittles any and all positions she's had in the past. Say what you want about Hillary, but she's been a state senator and the Secretary of State. But the first thing that comes up is that she was the wife of a president.

Historically, we are accustomed to seeing men in leadership positions. Think about the number of times you've boarded a plane. Now think about how many times you've heard a woman announcing, "This is your captain." I can recall once hearing a female. Luckily (but unfortunately), it was during my adulting years, so I thoroughly appreciated being in the comfort of a woman's hands. I'm sure some people aboard may have thought, "Dear Lord, we're gonna die" or "That must be the co-captain." Women at the helm are so uncommon that it's frightening when one gets there. Some people associate this fear with inexperience. That association with inexperience is their own inexperience, so they immediately doubt that she can pull off the job or jokes that she had to sleep with someone in order to get to the position she's in. Most don't think, "Damn! She did that! Must have been tough to get to be commander of this unit." It isn't just tough due to the standard requirements to get to the position, but also because of the added bullshit she had to endure because some men are assholes.[42] She certainly had to jump through unnecessary hoops just to prove that she is undeniably better than any of her male counterparts. To get to that position, she may have had to learn golf just so she wouldn't be left out of important decision-making conversations that are being discussed on the golf course. Or maybe she had to learn to love smoking cigars and drinking whiskey to have something to do after work with the team. Perhaps, she had to start watch dumb zombie shows just so she can join the

---

[42] Not all men. Just like...a lot of them.

conversation during lunch. Making it to that leadership position wasn't just about doing the required work. It was also being five times better than any man at it and learning extra shit she doesn't give a damn about.

During feminism conversation, chivalry is always brought up as a counterpoint. Let me give you a very brief history on chivalry, or the chivalric code, and how it fits into our perception of feminism today.

Chivalry was created during medieval times to describe the religious, moral, and social code in which knights would follow. The chivalric code is what made a man a knight. Throughout the years, this code stood in place to show how a man should conduct himself. This was very prominent when young men would present themselves to a woman and her family. There was a code of conduct upon which a man should handle women to ensure she and her family could trust that he would do his duties as a man. Namely, to protect her as a knight would. Therefore, chivalry was created because men didn't know how to act and needed instructions!

According to Merriam-Webster, the definition of chivalry is "courteous behavior, especially that of a man towards women." I say it's high time to get rid of the "especially that of a man towards women" part. Chivalry is simply courteous behavior. I'm sure you can think of a time where you've held a door for someone. Regardless of your gender, this simple act of kindness is a form of chivalrous behavior. Chivalry isn't just something men can do. It's something we all do.

Feminism will continue to change, just like it changed from bra burning to what it is today. And as it changes, so will people; some will hop on over to embrace feminism, some will go the other way, and some will remain in the middle. What is important to remember is that no matter where you stand, embrace the change. When we encounter someone that isn't a feminist, don't shame them. Find out more information. Understand what piece you may be missing, or what piece they may be.

Oftentimes, we find it hard to embrace change due to the need to be entirely right about an issue. The issue that hinders us from embracing change is that we believe we are 100 percent right and there is no room for doubt. We talk over each other and ignore that person's perspective because "they are wrong." If everyone is wrong, who's right? Accepting that we may learn something new is what happens when you open yourself up to listen to someone else's point of view. You actually may be wrong, or you may find an angle you never considered before.

It's easy to go into a conversation knowing that you have the same viewpoints. What happens when you are bomb shelled that your bestie is not a feminist? Do you hound him until he becomes one, or do you listen to his perspective and allow him to make his own decision? It's easy to say the latter, but sometimes our natural reaction is, "WTF?! Who ARE you!? How did we get this far in life and you never shared this information?!"

We also need to allow people to have a past where they were wrong. We say we want people to change, but when they do change, they still get bullied for their mistakes of the past. We need to recognize when people change and believe them. Speaking from personal experience, once we know someone to have a stance, it's hard for us to accept anything else. We've already bound that person into a certain box. Yet, when we change, we expect people to believe it immediately. It shouldn't be a one-way street. We should allow people to grow and show growth. Showing growth means they may slip up, but they can correct themselves. Don't shame them and hold it against them.

7

pay it forward

When I was in graduate school, I was in a regular apartment and rent was due on the first. It was considered late after the fifth of the month. For whatever HBCU reason, one month my financial aid didn't come through in time for me to pay my rent. I didn't know how I was going to pay. I didn't have a job. My family was living check to check, so forking over money to pay someone else's rent wasn't really in the budget. Being a very prideful person, I didn't reveal to many people that I was in this financial bind.

During a routine visit to a professor's office, I mentioned that I had this problem, but assured her that I'd figure something out. She asked me, "Like what?" I had no comeback. I was stumped. If I knew a solution, I'd probably have done it already. She looked at me and said, "How much is your rent?" I immediately started to refuse the money. She waited for me to stop refusing something she hadn't offered and asked again, "How much is your rent?" I told her, "Five fifty." She looked at me like I'd told her $5.50. She was like, "That's it? I'll give it to you. No refusing." I had no rebuttal to someone saying you can't refuse. I just exclaimed that I would pay her back as soon as I could.

About two weeks later, my financial aid pushed through and I was able to pay her back. I put all five hundred and fifty dollars in an envelope and headed to her office. I waited until we were alone to pull out the envelope. Damn near in tears, I explained how I appreciated her helping me out, and I don't know how I would have done it without her kindness. Then I handed her the envelope. She pushed the envelope back and said, "You don't have to pay me back." I was bewildered, and tried again, saying, "No, thank you for your help." She refused again. I tried again. She refused with the caveat, "You keep it. Just promise me you will pay it forward." At the time, I didn't know what that meant, but I exclaimed, "Consider it done!"

What she did for me that day reaffirmed my faith in humanity. I didn't tell any student that she'd done it for me since she'd clearly trusted in my discretion. Also, I knew if other people found out they would expect the same from her, and that wasn't fair. Although I wanted to shout it out to the world, I would only generally mention how she helped me. I'd say, "She helped me out in a really tough spot and I'm extremely grateful."

It wasn't until years later, when I was presented with the same situation, that I understood. I had a friend call me in tears because she had no idea how she was going to pay her rent. Some political bullshit prevented her from getting her full paycheck. Although I wasn't ballin' outta control, I did have enough money to solve her problem. I recalled my professor's charge, and I leapt at the opportunity. I told my friend that

I could help her pay her rent. When she hesitated, I completely understood what she was feeling. The struggle between the overwhelming relief that your problem was solved and the ever-present feeling that you are being a burden on someone, plus the fact you have no idea how you will pay them back. At some point, you realize that you have no other (legal) options, so you accept. It doesn't come until later that you are hit with the thought that someone loves and trusts you enough to pay one of the largest bills that you have.

Paying it forward doesn't have to come in the form of monetary contributions. It simply means to give back to someone that isn't the original giver. And as a student, recent graduate, or just mid-twenty-year-old, paying it forward will come in a variety of gifts, perhaps even a compliment. Compliments are my favorite. I love giving them. I compliment people because it feels good to receive a compliment. We all love receiving compliments but why not give them as well? It's easy to give compliments to people that we know. Why not dish them out to people we don't know? Imagine the feeling of receiving a compliment, especially from someone who doesn't have to speak to you at all. Think about it; someone has to go out of their way to first get your attention, then say something to you when they didn't need to, and thirdly for it to be nice! That's a lot in a world where we literally walk on top of each other. I challenge you to compliment a stranger today. Just say one nice thing to someone you don't know, and I promise their smile will make you want to do it again. Don't know what to say? Here are some examples, which are all unisex, light, and can hardly be construed as something sexual:

- That's a nice [enter clothing article].

- You look lovely today.

- Those shoes are NOICE!

- That's a dope hat.

- Clean haircut.

- Dope glasses!

- I'm digging that sweater.

- You're walking with confidence this morning!

Now I know the rebuttal that often comes for not paying it forward: it can lead to being taken advantage of. It's true. That might happen and you have to be aware enough to know if and when it is happening. But that's no excuse because we can only ever control our own actions, never anyone else's. There's a rule that illustrates this perfectly and though I'm not religious, I live by it:

Do unto others as others...shit I don't remember it... Basically, treat people the way you want to be treated.

I attempt to live by that rule because I think it's a good rule. I think it is the foundation of every religion, and every good person. If you do things for other people that you want done to you, then you can rarely go wrong. (Obviously, there are some exceptions.) I've recently had someone tell me that I go above and beyond what any friend would do.

This person didn't mean it to be a compliment. Quite the opposite actually. The infliction in their voice was accusatory. They didn't like that I would leap bounds for people that wouldn't do the same for me. I explained to him that I made that choice a while ago, and. that I would treat people the way I'd want to be treated. I think I'm a fucking queen, so I treat others like royalty. I know that it will be rare that I find multiple people that treat me like that queen I am. However, that's my choice. I am aware that I may get used. Nevertheless, I can't control how someone decides to treat me, just how I decide to treat others. I believe I am conscious enough to know when I am being taken advantage of, and that I can handle it accordingly. I am also fortunate to have people in my life that care about my well-being, and that they will call out the bullshit.

I've decided to live a life of positivity and giving. While recognizing that I cannot pay it forward in every situation nor can I give a helping hand to everyone that needs one, I do try to live a good life. I live a life knowing that I did something positive for another human in hopes that that positive thing will inspire them to do the same for someone else. Even the smallest of compliments are still an act of kindness that can butterfly effect into a world of change.

8

not just you

Being a young woman is difficult, regardless of race or religion. As a woman you go through many physical changes. Some of those changes you learn from class or your parents. Other changes you learn from your friends. But then there are things that we go through and we don't know if it's just us that's dealing with it. We're too embarrassed to bring it up, so we just accept it as something that happens and keep moving.

Believe it or not, periods are a perfect example. Sure, every girl and woman know that they aren't the only ones that have them, but what happens during those periods is very rarely discussed. No woman wants to let slip something she thinks is abnormal for fear of being the oddball out. Growing up, I was taught to hide my period from the world. I had the talk with my mother in a room where it was just me and her. She gave me her tips and tricks on how to conceal my pad or tampon. During this talk she consoled me because I was crying for no reason. She informed me that what was happening to me was natural. She told me that this means that

I am a woman and that every woman goes through this. When I got old enough (or when my mother decided she wasn't going to do it anymore), I ventured off to the drugstore to purchase feminine products. I felt embarrassed to make the purchase and I bought extra shit to make it seem like it wasn't for me. I may have even purchased the light products because I didn't want the cashier to think I had blood gushing out of my hooha. From that point forward, I spoke about my period as if I was a part of a secret society; to other members, behind locked doors, and in whispers.

regulating • your • emotions

Now that we've talked about periods, we have to talk about emotions. As much as we try to deny it, females are emotional creatures. Genetically, we tend to be more emotionally stimulated than men. Throughout society, we have been perceived to be inept in stressful situations because of our emotions. Due to this perception, we are treated as, for lack of a better word, inferior. Many of us have noticed that we are treated this way, and it frustrates us to no end. For those that haven't experienced it yet, you will. We've heard it time and time again that females make irrational decisions because of their emotions. We can't deny that sometimes we are motivated by involuntary emotions. I hate these emotions. I hate when I suddenly start crying because I'm mad. I get even more angry; it makes me cry even harder. I hate that I was just at the dentist, and when she hit a nerve, I was crying. Not a boo-hoo sob, but that silent tear fall shit. Inwardly, I was like "Ouch, that hurt. Fuckin' drill." I was fine; I just felt the drill and that wasn't fun. It wasn't a big deal. Outwardly, however, my emotions portrayed made it seem as if the dentist just murdered my dog in cold blood right in front of me. It wasn't the tear that made me upset. It was the knowledge that I was about to cry and couldn't stop myself. I felt that feeling right behind your nose and eyes, when you are stimulating the tear ducts, and knew what was about to happen. I was willing my body into shutting that shit down. The tears were like, "Nah... Imma do me right now." I told the dentist I needed a minute, and while she and the hygienist watched, a single tear trickled down my right cheek. Immediately, everyone became extremely awkward and apologetic. I knew that if I tried to console them and let them know I really was ok; the tears would take that as their opportunity to hold my throat hostage. I would choke on any words that came out. I opted not to speak, but to just hold one finger up. I sat in the dentist chair and silently cried for about two minutes. I didn't try to fight it. I may have even had the "bitch, please" face. As I sat there crying, I thought, "This is the fuckin' shit I'm talking about. Emoting for no damn reason."

As a feminist it irks me to say this, but most of the time, it's our Premenstrual Syndrome (PMS). Just for the sake of it, we deny that anything to do with PMS. It's a natural reaction to reject the suggestion that any of our emotions are a result of PMS. Especially if a man suggests it. However, if we are honest with ourselves, sometimes it is. PMS has a variety of symptoms including mood swings, tender breasts, food cravings, fatigue, irritability, and depression. Because I knew that PMS had such a bad connotation, I was willfully ignorant of its existence. I just assumed I didn't get it and fought anyone that implied that I had it. It wasn't until I was at work one day, and a new co-worker, Dan, came over to help me fix my computer. The other guys on my team knew that I liked to solve my own problems and that if I really needed help, I'd ask for it. This new guy insisted on helping me. I went back and forth with him, and then just gave up because I was getting unreasonably angry. Even after the situation was over, I was still fuming over it for the next two hours! I had a meeting with myself and said, "Self. WTF is wrong with you? Why are you still upset over this? It's over with. There is no logical reason for you to still be upset right now." Yet, I was still angry and frustrated with him. I took a step back to ask myself what reason would cause this lingering anger. Did I not like this particular employee? No, he's new and he was just trying to help. Was I jealous of his abilities? Nah! I'm fuckin' awesome, and he wants to be me! That's when it dawned on me. I'm fuckin' PMS-ing right now! Several things ran through my head. First, "SHIT! PMS is real." I could no longer ignore its existence. Second, this is a disadvantage. I need to get in front of this. Third, I fuckin' hate Dan now. Fourth, let me put this on my calendar. I want to track this.

Whether you're in college or working, this natural female phenomenon can always be a disadvantage. It's too easy to brand female workers as irrational or overly emotional, and it is impossible to blend in so well that gender will not be a factor. Even when I decided to use a tracker, I quickly realized that it was no match for PMS. It seems your body tends to react in ways that doesn't have anything to do with the current situation. It's like your body just has had enough of whatever, and just breaks the fuck down.

The only thing I could do to combat PMS was learn how to "handle" my emotions. The best way to combat these emotions is to be aware when I'm emoting differently. It takes time and self-awareness, but it's possible. Sometimes it's just a day of emoting. Sometimes it's a week. When I PMS, everyone fuckin' frustrates me. They don't just frustrate me. They *fuckin'* frustrate me. People's presence makes me want to punch babies. My emotions are on ten. When I take off my bra, my nipples feel like someone has been pinching them all damn day. I feel extra fat and sloppy. I don't want to wear makeup because I give zero fucks. I don't want to work out. I just want to come home to my chocolate peanut butter graham crackers, get in the bed, watch Netflix, and not communicate with anyone. PMS is real and a whole bitch.

When I realize that I'm emoting, I try to stay away from and not talk to as many people as possible. This proves to be quite difficult since I have a real job that I go to Monday through Friday. You find out how little you actually need to say at work when you decide not to interact with people. (You can also get a lot done!) I've mastered the art of smiling and nodding. Now don't get me wrong, I have had my emotions get the best of me at work. I have grabbed my hair and demanded a co-worker "Get out my cube." Then the jackass just stepped over the threshold and continued to squabble with me. My emotions told me, "Girl, we don't need this job, just go punch him in the face." However, my brain knew better and talked me out of it. Deep breaths. The whole counting to ten bullshit. I do that. In that time, I'm able to rationalize things just enough to keep my job. I did go back to that co-worker and apologize. He didn't realize that I was annoyed but it was unprofessional of me and I needed to clear it up.

Realizing when you are PMS-ing and learning to manage it will take time, requires focusing on your emotions and analyzing which emotions are real and which are heightened. Hopefully learning about my experiences and my strategies will help you to identify your emotions the next time you find yourself experiencing a heighten emotional period.

I try to help my fellow female co-workers and friends on how to manage their emotions, especially at work. The key is to realize it's not personal and to step back and consider the situation for a non-victim point-of-view. You'll learn that you are probably overreacting. It's not about you all the time. (see No One Cares).

periods

Just a forewarning that this section of the chapter will be very graphic. If you don't want to know any additional information about periods, please skip this chapter. However, I think that a lot of information here will help you feel...normal.

Historically, women where taught to find different ways to exist without making men uncomfortable. Therefore, generation after generation women were taught to hide their periods from the world.

In grade school, the students were separated according to gender to learn about their bodies. I recall that fateful day in fourth grade when we segregated the class. Boys on the right, girls on the left. We filed into two distinctive lines and marched down to two different classrooms. Till this day, I don't know what they told the boys. I do recall them showing us a video that involved a mother showing her daughter what a uterus looked like with pancake mix.[43] We learned how babies were made, what periods were and other things that were just between us girls.

As time passes, we are slowly learning that the female body is something that should be celebrated. That periods aren't the enemy. That we shouldn't have to hide them. That it shouldn't have to be a secret. Keeping it a situation "just between us girls" is quite ignorant. Guys need to know just as much about a female's body as she does. At some point in a guy's life he is going to have to interact with a woman. That woman is going to have a period. Sometimes that woman is also going to be a person that he wants to have sex with. At some point, that period is going to be a topic of discussion.

Through my experience, I've learned that guys know very little about a period. They rely on the female to be fully informed and handle any issues that may arise. Long ago, I was casually involved with a guy that deployed for 45 days at a time. Every time before he left, we would schedule a hook-up date. One time I told him that I wouldn't be able to hook up with him. He was baffled. I informed him I'd be on my period around that time. He once again was perplexed as to how I knew this information so far in advance. I decided to take a screenshot of my "period app". He had *several* questions. The first being, "You keep track of your

---

[43] To this day, I've never poured pancake mix in the pan with pipette...I'm pretty sure no one does it this way but I'm just saying, I was traumatized

period?" Hell, yeah dude! How old are you!? Why don't you know females keep track of this shit? We can't just have that bitch spring up on us.

The second question was, "How does it know though?" This is when I started thinking, this 30-something year old guy shouldn't be asking me these questions. "Am I sleeping with an idiot? Ugh, I hate dummies."

Luckily, I had time. I explained that a period typically happens every 28 days. They differ in how long they last depending on the person. Some women have 3-day periods while others can have 8-day cycles. Some women's cycles are heavy the first two days while others have blood flowing out of them like the ancient rivers of Babylon each day.

After I explained the basics of a female cycle to him, we went into the dynamics of the app. What do green circles mean? What about the blue? Safe and unsafe days. He texted back. All caps. WHAT!? I explain how there are days that I'm more likely to get pregnant and days I'm not. Some females want this information if they are trying to conceive. I am not one of those people. Hence why we use condoms.[44]

At the forefront of my mind, I thought, what an idiot? However, the longer I thought about it, I realized that socially there isn't any point in his life where someone forced him to learn this information. Any other girl that he had sex with probably didn't want to ruin the moment (or whatever the fuck) and pretending like her period wasn't important to

---

[44] Next time, we may need to double up because I can't get accidently pregnant by his dumb ass.

explain. Most guys just learn, if a girl says she's on her period, she can't have sex. No more questions needed. Outside of a sexual partner, the only other time a guy learned about a menstrual cycle was in high school health class. Learning any more about it would require him to go out and research the information on his own. Women barely want to do that so why would a guy voluntarily go out and find this information. That's just like women voluntarily finding more information about... I literally don't know an equivalent to use as an example here. So, I think his questions and ignorance is more of a rule than an exception.

Since the period is such a taboo topic, we grow up afraid to talk about the changes that are happening with our bodies. It is not uncommon for a young lady to assume that what is happening to her is abnormal and withhold the information from the world. I was one of those young ladies. I didn't know that things that were happening to my body were normal or abnormal until I was in college. I was fortunate to end up in a dorm with very open and confident women. I'd never been around females that weren't my mother or little sister. I would sit in their rooms and listen to their frank conversations about periods and sex and their vaginas. More often than not, I had nothing to contribute. I was inexperienced sexually and I wasn't in tune with my body enough to give any real contribution. So, I listened. Some of the more important things that I've learned are:

- There is extra pooping during your period. Just blood and poop everywhere!

- A tampon shouldn't hurt. You shouldn't feel it after it's inserted.

- There is some discharge that comes from your vagina.

- Wipe from front to back to avoid poop getting in your vagina.

- Your vagina discharges an odor a few days after your period.

- Damn near every girl has had a bloody pants story. Even as an adult.

- If you are sexually aroused, you discharge more than normal and that is what is meant by the term "getting wet."

These are things that were never discussed with me and I had to find out as I was growing into a new adult. Not everyone has a parent that is open enough to have such a conversation. After I found those things out, I felt normal. Knowing that I'm not the only one that excessively poops when I'm on my cycle is just one of the many things, I've learned that now allows me to live a less stressed life. I don't know if any of those things helped you feel normal, but I hope so.

pads • & • tampons

I just wanted to write a quick blurb on tampons. I mean since we are talking about periods, why not?

First off, tampons are the bee's knees. Whoever invented the tampon was a freaking genius. I imagine someone was like, "We need to put a stopper in this hole that keeps leaking blood." And boom, the tampon was invented! I assume that is an accurate description of an actual historic event.[45]

I remember when I first started my period, my mother asked me if I wanted to use tampons or pads. My immediate response was pad. My reasoning: at the time, I was not a proponent of sticking things up my vagina. (I have since reversed my position on this.) I thought that only sexually active people would be comfortable jamming a stick up their vag. At 12, I decided that after I become sexually active, I'll investigate tampons. So, I stuck with pads. Pads became the bane of my existence. During high school I spent an inordinate amount of time making sure that I didn't bleed through my jeans. Pads made being an athlete very difficult. Let me stop pretending that I was athletic. I was in the marching band. I wasn't even like an instrument playing member of the band. I was a flag girl. Whatever, that isn't the point. It's about trying to march with a diaper between your legs. There have been plenty of days when the pad that was supposed to be between my legs end up in the crevice of my butt or the front of my panties. The adhesive does nothing if you are a moist factory between your legs. Being overweight heated up the area way quicker. Blood, sweat, and general vagina juices. All in a pad that was good for 2 to 3 hours (according to the box).

In college, I began to get more and more interested in having sex. (Yes, I was a virgin in college.) I'd gotten it in my head that if I start

---

[45] I refused to investigate any further.

wearing tampons that I would be better prepared for the actual act. I wouldn't be nervous that a foreign object was entering my lady hole. I bought a cheap box of tampons. I remember they had a cardboard applicator and thick as shit! (Proof that they were the cheap ones.) I went in the communal bathroom. Lysol'd the toilet seat down then sat down. I opened the package and upon seeing this thick stick that was supposed to go inside of me, my eyes nearly popped out of my head. I braced myself and started to slide the tube inside. I was met with resistance. I recognized that was my body saying, "Bitch, what the fuck is that? Nah, I don't like it." I stopped. Took two deep breaths and tried again. My body gave way some. I finally got it in. I walked to the sink to wash my hands and that's when I felt it. It was like an uncomfortable rubbing. I didn't like it. I really didn't like it. I ran into the stall and ripped it out. I was like, Nope, not having sex. Yes, I just equated the uncomfortableness of a tampon to dismissing sex altogether.

A few months later, I was sitting in my best friend's room. Her room was the hub for all the other girls on the floor. I was observing the conversation; something I found myself doing often. On this particular day, the conversation led her roommate to say, "If your tampon hurts, it's not in all the way." My eyes got wide. Is that why mine hurt? This revelation made me want to try again. I still had my entire box of cardboard tampons so the next month, I tried again. I pushed it in as far as my body would take it. When I walked away this time, I was amazed! I didn't feel anything! Tampons are the tits!

Because of tampons, I have had fewer "accidents." Any accidents I have had were due to me forgetting to put in a tampon. Tampons are not as messy as a pad. Pads were like petri-dishes of blood. Now, just the thought of a pad with blood being pressed up against my vagina, makes me want to throw up a little.

I'm not hating on women that use pads. They are commonplace. You are more likely able to bum a pad off a 13-year-old than a tampon. I just thought I'd share my pad to tampon story, just in case your story is similar. You know that you aren't the only one that didn't like tampons. But I suggest you try it again. My reaction to tampons was exactly the same when I started using a razor. For the life of me, I don't know what I was using before to shave my legs and armpits. I'm sure it was me watching other females in my dorm use a razor that I was intrigued to use one. When I tell you that my leg was smoother than a baby's bottom... Changed my life! Again, #noShade for Team No Shave.

9

no one cares

This is probably the number one concept I like to share with my friends. I like to think that it helps them open up to the idea that they can do and be more. It's a pretty simple concept. It's not gender, race, age, or sexual orientation specific.

No one cares about you.

That's it. Five simple words.

Upon first glance you may think this is quite a harsh concept. On the contrary, it isn't. It's a new perspective. What would you do if no one cared about what you were doing? How would you act? How would you dress?

Well, I'm here to tell you that no one is looking at you. No one cares about you. No one cares what you do most of your day.

Now, obviously I'm not saying no one loves you, go kill yourself. I'm simply saying that every little thing you do is virtually undetected by other human beings. (I'm also not saying to have your own personal Purge Day.) People tend to not really focus on the things you are doing, because they are focused on the things *they* are doing!

Think back to the last time you were at the grocery store. Did you pay attention to anyone in the store? Everyone was just a blob that was either in your way or getting out of your way. You couldn't tell if they were male or female, silver, or blue. They could have been bucket nekkid and you wouldn't have noticed them! You didn't care about those people and they didn't care about you. If you bumped into someone you said excuse me and kept it moving.

The gym is another great example. "Get back to the gym" is probably the number one New Year's resolution. People put it on their list and get up the first Monday after New Year's (I mean who starts a resolution on a Thursday?!) to hit the gym. That's when they realize why they stopped going. Several people don't go to the gym because they don't want people looking at them. Whether they don't want people to see how awkward they are when they run on the treadmill, or how big they are trying to sit on the row machine, it comes down to people not wanting to be judged at the gym. Being a big girl myself, I felt the same way. I used to go to the gym at insane times of the day or night to avoid the crowd. When I did get the courage to go, I would strategically use equipment that no one else was around. I would not attempt to do more than I thought I could do (I didn't want witnesses seeing me fail). In my mind, I wouldn't use certain equipment because I didn't want someone to see me and burst out laughing. Had I realized that no one cared about me, I would have spent more time in the gym instead of rushing through my set, in fear of being the source of someone's viral video.

Looking back, I wish I had someone come up to me and say, "Hunnie. No one cares if you are here." I'd probably smile at her underneath my embarrassment and pretend like I'd just wrapped up my last set, then go home for the day. That's the type of person I was then.

Now that I "gym,"[46] I know that most people go to the gym with headphones. They are typically rocking out to music or listening to an audiobook. Their mind is probably on how many deadlifts they can do, or which exercise they are going to do next. If you are anything like me, you are thinking, "Why the fuck haven't I died yet? I can't breathe! Jesus! Come get me!" Basically, what I'm trying to say is no one cares about you. No one is focused on what you have going on. Everyone is so focused on themselves that they don't have time to focus on anything that you are doing. We are so self-aware of what we are doing that we think that everyone else is as well. This isn't meant to be a blanket statement to excuse you from the consequences of your actions but more so permission to be free to be yourself; do what makes you happy without the fear of being judged.

Just think of all the people that you've walked by and haven't acknowledged. For some reason, we think that other people think extremely differently than we do. Generally, people think the same way.

---

[46] I like to make nouns into verbs.

One of my favorite things to say to people think they'll be judged is, "What would you do if you saw someone else doing it?" More than likely they will say that they wouldn't give it much mental space. That's when I'll ask, "Why do you think it'll be different for you?" What we don't say aloud is that we think everyone is thinking about us. That we are special. Once you accept that you aren't special, and that every person you encounter doesn't think about you as much as you think about yourself, you will start to care less about how you are perceived. You can start "doing you."

Like a fine wine, it will take some time to build up this tolerance. You will have to take baby steps to really, truly start giving zero fucks about what someone else thinks. It's funny that we have had the "I give zero fucks about this" thought. But it's rare that we actually mean it. Giving zero fucks means that you are focused on you and your happiness at that moment. You are going to do things that make you happy, regardless of other people's opinions. Don't let some fictitious notion that your every move is being watched prevent you from shooting your shot.

sh!t life

Every woman should have some idea of what's going on with her finances. There are too many stories where a woman has been in a bind due to financial ignorance. In some cases, women are taken advantage of because they don't have the wherewithal to know more about their financial situation.

A public example of this is the story behind why Rihanna wrote *Bitch Better Have My Money.* Her accountant thought she was just another young and stupid woman that wasn't invested in her financial situation. So, he tried to take advantage of her. However, Rihanna is quite intelligent and had her finances audited. She learned she'd been cheated out of her money. In the end, the bitch got her money!

Another reason why we need to be more involved in our finances and not rely solely on someone else to manage our funds is in the event that person is no longer around, this is especially true if you are married.

You want to be able to manage things yourself. You want to be able to have some inkling of what's going on.

But finances can be daunting. They're complicated and messy, and it's no wonder that young adults are terrified. I used to hate the thought of having to manage my money. I didn't want to balance my checking account, and figure out how much to save to do x, y, and z. I got overwhelmed trying to figure out the best financial plan, investments, and all that bullshit.

The truth was, I was afraid of money. Money has been the downfall of some many people in my family. No one really knew how to manage their money. Bad spending habits trickled down from generation to generation. My mom used to say, "Robbing Peter to pay Paul." Essentially, it means using the money for one bill to pay another. I based my understanding about money on what I learned from the people around me and the experiences they had. This wasn't uncommon in the Black household.

Growing up in my community, it was fucking impossible to find someone that knew anything about finances. Schools didn't teach us about finances, and they still don't. Most person had to figure it out on our own. That's why the cycle continued. My goal is to break that cycle. I want to give you some advice that I wish I learned early on, and to show you that learning about finances doesn't have to be so scary.

10 payday loans

Asking for help is not the easiest thing to do, in particular if you are seeking financial assistance. Typically, when someone reaches out to a resource for help, they've come to their last resorts. Two of the most common resource options are asking family members and short-term loans.

Growing up in a low-income community, I saw firsthand the type of financial decisions made by people that were deprived of financial stability. Frequently, if someone came upon twenty dollars in their pocket, it wouldn't stay in their pocket for long. It was routine that within the first hour, the money was already spent.

Low-income communities are so deprived of money that they fantasize what they will spend the money on prior to receiving it. The basic thought process is, "Let me feed my immediate need." Coming into a large sum of money at one time is the ultimate goal. Therefore, tax season and the lottery are prevalent in low-income communities. The economy preys on low-income consumers to feed that immediate want when they receive tax refunds, and to purchase amenities before necessities.

The paycheck-to-paycheck lifestyle is when all or most of your monthly income covers your monthly expenses with no money left over for savings. As a child, I assumed that everyone lived that way. I was confused as to how else one could live. In my world, I wasn't cognizant of savings accounts or retirement plans. Usually, you had a plan for the money before you received it. There was never a money surplus.

One countermeasure to a financial lull is a short-term, high-interest loan. These loans are commonly known as a payday or title loan. Back at home, they were just a stone's throw away from each other. For those that are privileged enough to never have had to get a payday loan, let me spell out what it entails. These loans present themselves as fast and easy ways to get a little extra money before your next paycheck. It surely is. However, they prey on individuals that have deep financial trouble.

Let me set the stage. You work in Virginia at the local Walmart. You earn three dollars above minimum wage; at the time of this writing that's $10.25 per hour.[47] You're living in a one-bedroom apartment which is approximately $755/month. Your gross paycheck is $980; let's say after taxes it's about $784. You get approximately $1568/month. Nearly one

---

[47] Why the fuck is minimum wage still $7.25!?

entire check will go towards your rent. Next you must pay for the essentials, electricity, water, phone, and a host of other things. After all the bills are paid, you realize you don't have any money for food and gas, so you seek out a payday loan.

I looked to find a popular payday loan company. This company advertises a 14-day one-hundred-dollar loan with an APR of 688.28%!

Bitch, what!? Why would I ever want to get this loan? I mean, I don't know what APR is but that doesn't even sound right...688.28%!

I've sort of misled you for dramatic effect.[48] The interest rate of 688.28 percent is annually. APR stands for Annual Percentage Rate. If your loan were to be outstanding for a year, then you would pay nearly seven times the originally borrowed amount. However, if you just borrow it for fourteen days, you'll only pay about 26.4 percent.

Hearing 26.4 percent interest is meaningless to someone with no idea of what is considered a good interest rate. The concept of a "good" interest rate can vary depending on what you are purchasing. If you were approved for a car loan with 11 percent interest may sound fantastic when you compare it to the 26.4 percent previously mentioned. This is until you hear that someone else was approved for a car loan at 1.5 percent.

You may think twenty-six percent on a payday loan isn't too bad. If you borrow $100 it's just $126.40. Just $26.40 extra. True. But

---

[48] Sorry, not sorry

remember, you didn't have enough money last month after paying for your essentials. This month you not only have to pay those bills, but now you need to subtract $126.40 off top! If you make $784 the next two weeks, then you've already started the new two weeks off with $657.60. You are not in a perpetual cycle of never having enough. Welcome to payday loan!

Since payday loan companies are trash and take advantage of people who are already at their wits end, they have additional fees.

What do you mean by 'additional fees'?

I'm glad you asked. No ID? There's a fee. A new customer? There's a fee. No Payday Loan ID? There's a fee. No check? There's a fee. No bank accounts? There's a fee. I couldn't make this stuff up if I tried! Talk about kicking you when you are down!

I'm not faulting anyone whose remedy is a payday loan. We must do what we need to survive. I just want to open your eyes to what you could possibly get into by taking one out. Some people aren't aware an don't look at these types of loans. Some just see them as an immediate solution when it should be a last resort.

11

stay in your lane

Social media entices us to show off our best life. When we see others living their best life, it tempts us to 'one-up' them. If Steven gets a new jacket, it lures Tom into getting the jacket AND the matching fedora. We want to show that we make the most money, go on the best vacations, drive the best car, or get the biggest house.

Imagine you are out at a club with your friends. Everyone's drinking and having a great time. Suddenly you yell, "Next round's on me." Your friends cheer! They toast to you! **In my best Quinta B. voice** You got monnney!

The next morning in your drunken stupor, you locate your wallet where you stuffed last night's receipt in with your credit card. Your tab was $110! Bitch, what?! You scan the receipt to see ten shots of Patrón which were nine dollars each. Ten?! It was only eight of us! Oh, yeah, we did meet that random couple. Nine dollars for a fucking shot! What the fuck?! **In a sadder Quinta B voice** You ain't got monnney.

Your one night of grandiose cost $110. You were living the high life, but now you must face reality. You now have a $110 bill that you are responsible for, simply because you wanted to create an illusion that you live a grandiose lifestyle. At the end of the day, you are responsible for the bill. You have to pay for this lavish lifestyle you've concocted to manipulate your friends. This is something that happens frequently to young adults. It's a lesson that is often learned the hard way.

I had a friend, let's call him Tobias, who constantly made awful financial decisions all in the name of impressing others. When we became friends, I had no idea that he made poor financial decisions. One day, shortly after I'd purchased my new car, we went for a ride and he constantly praised me on my new purchase. He revealed to me that he was interested in leveling up, but he was having some financial issues. Throughout our conversation, I learned he'd gotten advice from other people. As he told me what they said, I recognized that all advice isn't good advice. His friends were telling him that once he pays off a bill then he could use that extra money to buy new things. This advice he was getting was going to put him further into debt but allow him to still pose as if he was doing well. It didn't have his financial interest in mind, just his social status.

One of the issues Tobias presented me with was centered around his car. A year ago, he'd purchased a car, but was unhappy with it. He wanted to trade it in for the same car with upgraded features. He went back to the dealer, and they were accommodating. He received his first car payment, and that's when he learned he was paying a Lexus price tag for a Honda Civic! He was so focused on getting a vehicle to impress people that he didn't pay attention to the terms and conditions.

That wasn't the issue with his car, that was just the background story! Since he was paying upward of $700 for a Honda Civic, he wanted to lease an Infiniti. Additionally, he was upset that his girlfriend he'd been dating for two months wouldn't co-sign on the loan. Bruh!

He looked to me to co-sign, and I laughed in his face and disrespectfully declined. He tried to convince me that it was nothing but signing a document. I told him how cosigning a loan meant that I would be financially responsible for that loan if he didn't pay. I gently let him know that I wouldn't co-sign on a loan for anyone short of my mother (and I'd even question that decision). I wished him luck on his quest, and that was one of the last conversations he and I had.

That story brought up three topics I want to dive a little deeper on: financial advice, leasing a car, and financial habits.

financial • advice

When it comes to financial advice, there are a few questions you should ask yourself when getting advice from someone:

- Are they in a better financial state than me?
- Are they older and telling me what they wished they'd done?

- Do they rarely complain about financial problems?

If you answered yes to any of these, then more than likely you should listen to this person. This person has done the proper research or has the right life experiences to tell you things that help you in your financial life. However, never take advice at face value. Shit! Ask someone about the advice that I'm giving you in this book. [49]

leasing • a • car

For those that don't know, leasing a car essentially means "rent a car." The only people I think should lease a car are:

- People who like brand new cars
- People who don't drive too often

To start I must state, I've never leased a car. I don't see any value in leasing a car. I do know some people that have leased a car. The most common reason I hear is that they like to get a new car quite often. Some people want to keep their car payments low. Those who lease are comfortable with never actually owning their vehicle. They have come to terms that they will always have a car payment and willing to accept that.

Here is a list of pros and cons to leasing:

---

[49] For more information about mentors and advice, see Dots & Circles

Pros:	Cons:
No or low-down payment	Excess mileage penalties
Usually covered by warranty	Fees for excessive wear and tear
Lower monthly payments	Early lease termination fees
No upfront sales tax fees	Generally higher insurance premiums
No depreciation concerns	Monthly payments

When I learned about leasing, the topic of concern for me was the excessive mileage fee. When you rent a car[50], you have to stay under a set number of miles each year, which you determine at the start of your lease. If you return the vehicle with more miles than originally agreed upon, you must pay *per* mile. This price is about twenty cents per mile. This isn't bad if you go over like 10-20 miles, but most people go over hundreds or thousands of miles. Let's say your 3-year lease agreement is 10,000 miles per year. You average about 13,000 per year. That's a total of 9000 miles at $0.20/mile. You now have to pay an extra $1800 at the end of your lease. That's in additional to your monthly payments.

f i n a n c i a l • h a b i t s

We all want things that we shouldn't buy. How many times have you picked something up only to look at the price and regretfully put it back? Here's a good rule of thumb that I use: if I can't stop thinking about

---

[50] I should probably stop saying "rent a car", but that's what you are doing.

it after a week, then I can start ***thinking*** about getting it. Not get it but think about getting it. There are many things to consider. Can I afford it? Do I really need it? Where will I put it? Does it need any supplement things that will cost money? If not, am I willing to make the proper life adjustments to afford it? Don't let your desire overpower your judgement.

Changing your financial habits is just like going on a diet; it's a lifestyle change. Sure, you can do it for a little while with some results, but if you aren't fully dedicated, then you are just going to slip back into your regular habits. I'm not saying to go without eating. I'm saying don't buy those Prada shoes because just they have Prada written on the bottom.

At the end of the day, you are responsible for your bills. Whether you live your best life but have a bust bank account, or if you live a modest lifestyle with a banging bank account, you have to pay your bills either way. Your bills are yours, so be smart about what you spend your money on.

12 credit

Credit was always an expletive in my community. Credit equated to credit cards, which equated to debt, which equated to poor. No one thought of credit as a positive thing. Everyone I knew that had credit cards had an abundance of them. They'd damn near maxed out all of them and were struggling to keep up on the monthly payments.

For most people, college is when they get their first credit card. I got mine at that time. And most students don't know the first thing about credit cards or credit in general. I didn't, but I had read all the documentation that everyone throws away. I was terrified that I would end up with insane debt for the rest of my life.

For the most part, I used my card fairly responsibly. However, since I was still in college, my funds were low, and it was difficult to pay the bill. My mom would make payments on it for me sometimes, but it inevitably approached the credit limit. I managed to get about four new cards. One I saved to furnish my first apartment. About three years after getting my first credit card, I'd become the statistic that I'd fought so hard to avoid. I'd maxed out all of my credit cards and was overwhelmed on how I would repay my debt.

With $5000 of debt, I decided that I wanted to change my credit score from a 550 to an 850. My first step was contacting a debt consolidation company. Their policy required any card that was attached to the program would be closed. I added all but one. That one had a fairly low balance, and I kept it because I'd talked myself into believing that I needed it for "emergencies." With the program, instead of paying multiple credit card companies monthly, I paid the debt consolidation company a monthly payment which included a maintenance fee. The debt consolidation company would work with the credit card companies and determine how to divide my monthly payment between all the cards. The program would take five years to completely clear my debt. They gave me an amortization schedule, a table of how my loan should reduce over time with regular monthly payment. This helped me to understand how I would reduce my debt over the next five years.

I battled with the decision to use their services; I recognized that all they did was pay my credit cards for me. Even still, I proceeded to utilize their service. My reasoning was twofold: I needed to be forced into a situation that required me to start making better financial decisions, and I was enticed by having to make only one payment instead of multiple.

I vowed that I would not get myself in that situation again. During the five years in the program, I used that time to learn more about credit and how to use it to my advantage.

One of the first things I learned was about the debt-to-credit ratio. Essentially, you want to have more credit than debt. There is a

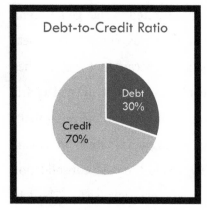

general rule of thumb to have no more than thirty percent debt -to- credit ratio.

This isn't a hard and fast rule, just a nice guide. You may have heard this line before, "No credit is worse than having bad credit." This is because you have more debt than credit. The more credit you have, the better it is because it tells providers a story on how much an institution trusts you to repay them.[51]

When I first got my credit card, I wanted the lowest credit limit possible; I didn't want to be tempted to spend more than that amount. This is the opposite of what you want. Credit card companies basically want to see if you are going to be tempted to spend all of the available credit available to you. You very well may do this, but to improve your credit score, you want to try to keep within the 70/30 ratio.

Once I learned this information, I changed my ways. First thing I did was determine my average monthly spend and calculate what number that was thirty percent of. With that amount in hand, I called the credit

---

[51] Side note: The Black Card famous folk talk about is issued by American Express. It is actually called the Centurion. It doesn't have a credit limit. Visa & Mastercard issue a Black Card as well but they are just luxury credit cards.

card company and requested that my credit limit be increased to this new credit limit.

---

t h e • m a t h

If my average monthly spend is $500, then the equation[52] would look like this:

$$New\ Credit\ Limit\ x\ 30\% = Average\ Monthly\ Spending$$
$$NCL \times 30\% = 500$$
$$NCL = \frac{500}{30\%} = \frac{500}{0.30}$$
$$NCL = 1666.67$$

Unbeknownst to me at the time, I'd started my credit history the moment I decided that I would keep the "emergency" credit card. Originally, my plan was to keep the card until I'd resurrected my credit score, then I'd trash it. However, with five years under its belt, trashing the card would hurt me more than it would help me. I'd learned that credit history was another major factor in determining your credit score. It goes back to the trust factor. Imagine trusting someone with your car. Someone you just met is less likely to get the keys, but the longer you've known someone, the more trustworthy that person is to you and the likelier you are to trust them with your car.

---

[52] You should have already known that there was going to be math in this section.

Discovering I would take a huge hit if I'd closed my card, I looked more into the card. I saw that they were charging me a 29.9 percent APR! That's payday loan rates! I immediately called to find out why. They informed me that it was due to *one* late payment two years prior! I was in a quagmire! I wanted to close the card, but I couldn't! I decided that I'd just get another card and completely stop using that card but keep it open.[53]

And that, my friends, is how I technically only have two credit cards. Of those two credit cards, I only use one. That card I use for daily use. Before Debt Consolidation 2004, I would only use my card for major purchases, like things I couldn't afford with my regular bank account. Now I use my card for everyday purchases. My motivation is twofold. First being that it's safer and more secure. I no longer walk around with cash in my pocket, but I hold a card that will protect me from a purchase if I can't get a resolution from the company. It also typically has additional services that can protect you when traveling.

The second motivator is to gain reward points. Reward points are points rewarded for every dollar you spend. Credit card companies allow you to redeem these points for cash back, gift cards or travel. Reward points seem like something only people with luxurious lives can take advantage of. This is simply not true. I initially used my points to fuel my Starbucks habit, but later I started getting into other things points could offer me. I have backpacked through Europe using my points.

---

[53] I just checked the card and 16 years later with a 830 credit score the APR is 22.24%. Fuck you!

The initial hunt for a rewards card can be daunting. You don't know what you are doing, what to look for, or if you want cash back or travel points. Like everything else in the world, it all depends on the individual. If you want to dive into reward point, I suggest starting with a card that issues gift cards. You can find which gift cards they offer before you sign up for the card. You can do like I did and use reward points to fund your habit. Mine happened to be Starbucks. After collecting enough points, I could redeem them through the credit card site for a $50 gift card. Score!

However, if you are someone that can keep track of different promotional seasons, maybe getting a card that offers higher rewards during a rotating schedule is good for you. If you like to travel, getting a card that has travel rewards is more beneficial. Personally, I want the easiest program possible. I don't want to have to remember that it's home improvement season, which starts in April and ends in June, so I get 3 percent cash back at home improvement stores, but 1 percent at groceries, blah blah blah. That's way too much for me to remember.[54] I found a card that offered something like, no annual fee the first year, five times the points on every purchase and 40,000 points as a signing bonus. Those 40,000 points are only given if you spend a certain amount of money in a short time frame. Typically, it's 40,000 points if you spend $4000 in the first three months. To spend $4000 in three months, you either have to use it for every purchase, or intend to spend a high volume very soon.

---

[54] For me, it's on the same level as extreme coupon clippers. For someone else, that's their jam.

When looking at reward cards, the higher the annual fee, the more rewards you reap.

To help control my debt, I decided to try to pay off my card by the end of every month. This isn't something I was able to do immediately. The idea of paying off your card monthly, especially if you put everyday purchases on it, means that you need to be prepared to see an extremely high bill at the end of the month. I have a friend that pays off his card on a weekly basis. This may be a solution to work up to a monthly payment. Personally, I can't remember to do anything every week. I did toy with the idea of getting a charge card. A charge card gives you all the securities of a credit card but requires that you have a zero balance at the end of the month. I chose to stick with the credit card due to the ability to retain a balance without penalty.

There's lots more that can be said about credit and credit cards. I have found the information provided is a great foundational step. This will lead you towards a better understanding of credit and financial health.

13

everyday living

In this chapter, is a collection financial concepts and ideas that I wanted to share.

debt • snowball

If you have debt, albeit credit cards or loans, you should pay the smallest bill first. Why? Who gets overwhelmed by 5011 bills every month? **raises hand** By paying off the smallest bills first, you start to eliminate the number of bills you have. Once you've paid off a bill, don't start celebrating and spending that "new" money. Roll it over to another bill. Now you are paying more on a bill to get that paid off quicker. Keep doing this until you are debt free. This is commonly known as the Debt Snowball, which sounds like the opposite of what it is.

just • ask

Every six months, I go through my bills and verify that I'm paying the lowest possible price. Sometimes service companies have promotions that you qualify for, but they won't necessarily call you to let you know. If you call your cell phone company or cable company and plainly ask what they can do to lower your bill, they will help you.

Example: I was paying ninety dollars a month for my cell phone with 450 mins, unlimited text, and 2 GB of data. This was ridiculous. I analyzed how much data I used and home much phone time I needed. When I called, I just said, "What can you do to lower my bill?" The agent looked through what promotions they had. As a single user on a plan, the standard plans were still pretty pricey. The agent suggested I go with a prepaid plan. I had reservations about a prepaid plan due to the stigma that prepaid plans were for people that couldn't afford a "real" account. However, after looking more into it, prepaid plans are the bee's knees! I now have unlimited minutes & text, and 10 GB of data for fifty dollars, no contract. For me, 10 GB of data is adequate. I don't mind connecting to Wi-Fi when necessary. During the winter holidays are typically the only time I go over my data. Even with the overage, I am still paying less yearly.

Try this with nearly any bill that you have.

---

re-evaluate

Seriously, sit and think about the bills that you have. Do you really need to have all your recurring bills?

The main bill that is commonly re-evaluated these days is the cable bill. Firstly, I'd like to point out that your TV works without cable. I didn't know people didn't know this. They've been so privileged to have cable that this is just a standard bill like water. I divert. Many shows come on a streaming app or a standard broadcasting website that most of the shows you watch can be seen online. As long as you don't mind waiting a day to see the show.

Maybe you can link up with a *reliable* friend and combine some of your services and get the family plan. Cell phones and music apps are known to have family plans. The family plans tend to have a discounted price plan.

---

a d v a n c e

When possible, try to get one month ahead of your bills. This gives you a nice cushion should something unexpected happen. This can take some time to do, especially when you're just starting out in a new job, so don't panic if you can't do this right away. You will have to pay double that bill in one month in order to get a month ahead. Take it slow and start with the lowest bill first. Some bills you can't prepay (mortgage, for example). Everything else, double up! Even rent if you can!

---

c r e d i t • r e p o r t

There are agencies that collect and researches your credit information which they sell to companies to help determine if you should be granted a loan. These agencies are called credit bureaus. The three main bureaus in the U.S. are Equifax, TransUnion and Experian. Luckily, you are entitled a free credit report from the three main credit bureaus every year. A rookie mistake is getting them all at the same time. I did this a couple of times and was pissed that they all said the same thing. I suggest that every trimester you pull a copy of your report. (Jan-May-Sept)

When you look at your report, make sure everything is on the up and up. What type of things should you look for?

- Unknown credit inquiries.
- Outstanding accounts.
- Open accounts that can be closed.
- Accounts opened without your permission.

c o s i g n i n g

Don't do it.[55]

l e n d i n g

---

[55] See chapter: stay in your lane

A common phrase I've heard is, "Don't lend what you can't lose."

Scenario: your cousin comes to you and asks for $200. You have $1000 in your emergency savings and $300 in your checking. What do you tell your cousin?

Correct Answer: "I don't have it to give."

You obviously can't take it out your checking because then you'll be left with $100, and now your cousin has more in their account than you. Your emergency savings is for that only. EMERGENCIES! Cousin's situation is not an emergency. Unless cuzzo is having a $200 life or death operation, you don't have it!

The next three chapters come directly from a blog that I created years ago. I wanted to dump all the information that I learned over the years somewhere in the hopes that someday I could create a book where I can disseminate this information. For me, the two major topics that I didn't understand but desperately wanted someone to teach me about were taxes and 401(k). I'd heard of these things, but I had no idea what they were or how they worked. In the following sections, you will get a beginner understanding of taxes, 401(k) and stocks. Just a forewarning, there are lots of numbers and math. I try to keep it simple.

14

taxes

They really should teach taxes in school. It's such an important aspect in your life. Here are just the few things I know about taxes.[56] I am at a place in my career where I am fortunate enough to have an accountant who prepares my taxes. It's beginning to get extremely complicated (and I like that I can blame someone else if they are messed up). However, before I had my accountant, I had to prepare my own taxes and figure out what was going on.

---

p e r s o n a l • e x e m p t i o n • f o r m

When you first get a job, one of the forms they have you fill out is called your Personal Exemption Form. If you've heard of someone ever

---

[56] Disclaimer: I live in Virginia so this information may be state specific.

talk about withholdings, that's what this form is. This form determines the amount of taxes that will be **withheld** from your check. It asks how many people you are financially responsible for, dependents. Some people put more dependents than they actually have so more taxes can be taken out of their checks. This is done so they can receive a bigger tax refund. They will receive a larger tax refund since they overpaid in taxes throughout the year. For me, this is the shittiest savings account ever. It's a way for people to force themselves to save money, but that money isn't collecting interest throughout the year. Highly not recommended.

Some people put fewer withholdings than they actually have so they can get more throughout the year. While I understand some people may need to do this to survive daily, this isn't a good idea either. Essentially, this approach backfires since you'll have to pay that money back in a lump sum at the beginning of the year. Again, highly not recommended and more unrecommended than the shitty savings account. It is best to just list your actual withholdings to avoid any major surprises at tax time.

w - 2

The W-2 is a form that you should receive from every job you worked that year. You receive this form at the beginning of every year. This is what you need to file your taxes. Typically, companies' issue these between the beginning of January and the end of March. You should wait for all your W-2s before filing your taxes. If you don't get a W-2 from a company, either call that company and ask for your W-2, or you can file taxes and send an amendment when it comes in. Typically, sending the IRS an amendment requires you to fill out another tax form.

---

t a x • b r a c k e t

You heard Jay-Z talk about tax brackets all the time, but what are they really?

Rate	Taxable Bracket	Tax Owned
10%	$0 to $9,700	10% of taxable income
12%	$9,701 to $39,475	$970 plus 12% of the amount over $9,700
22%	$39,476 to $84,200	$4,543 plus 22% of the amount over $39,475
24%	$84,201 to $160,725	$14,382.50 plus 24% of the amount over $84,200
32%	$160,726 to $204,100	$32,748.50 plus 32% of the amount over $160,725
35%	$204,100 to $510,300	$46,628.50 plus 35% of the amount over $204,100
37%	$510,301 or more	$153,789.50 plus 37% of the amount over $510,300

2020 SINGLE TAXABLE INCOME CHART

Here are the brackets. Yep, there are only seven. This chart can change. If you are reading this, you definitely don't have to worry about the last three brackets. By that point, you already have an accountant working the numbers for you.

Ok, where to start?

First, understand that there are different tax brackets for single, married, and head of household. The chart above is for single taxpayers.

Single meaning not married.

Married meaning married.

Head of household meaning there are folks living in your house that can pay taxes, but you pay for most of the shit in the house (rent, insurance, food, etc.).

So how does this thing work? Btw, I hate numbers soooo...

Well I love numbers, soooo...sounds like we've got an issue. I used to be a teacher, so let me see if I can break it down.

Imagine this: you are a single person with no kids making **$50,000**. This puts you in the **22%** tax bracket. If you do the math right away, the first thing you think is "_That means $11,000 goes to taxes! So, I only make $39,000 after taxes._"

Nah. Not really.

The last column of the tabl is pretty important. It lets you kno what portion of your income will b taxed at that amount. Let's go back t our $50,000. The last colum suggests that you must break you money into tiers. In this case, yo need three tiers: 10 percent, 1 percent, and 22 percent. On the fir: tier, you pay 10 percent on the first

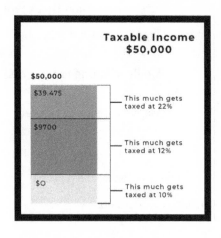

you pay 12 percent. This one is a little more complicated; you only pay 12 percent on the money that's more than $9701. but less than $39,475. That means that $29,775 is taxed at 12 percent. The final tier requires a 22% tax on anything over $39,475, which in this case is $10,525. That gives you a total of $6,858.50 paid in taxes.

Here is the formula:

$$es = (Max \times 10\%) + ((12\% \, Max - 10\% \, Max) \times 12\%) + ((Gross - 12\% \, Max) \times 22\%)$$
$$es = (9,700 \times 10\%) + ((39,425 - 9,700) \times 12\%) + ((50,000 - 39,425) \times 22\%)$$
$$es = (970) + (29,725 \times 12\%) + (10,525 \times 22\%)$$
$$es = 970 + 3,573 + 2,315.50$$

Is there a way to move to a lower tax or get more money but stay in the same tax bracket?

There are some things you can do to change what tax bracket you are in. These things are either tax credits or deductions. There are several things that are considered a tax credit or deduction. Here are a few of the more popular ones: Child Tax Credit, Adoption Credit, Student Loan Interest Deduction, and Medical Savings Account. You can also get deductions for medical/dental expenses, state and local taxes, home mortgage interest, casualty losses after a federal disaster, theft losses, job expenses, and charitable contributions.

Charitable contributions are probably one of the most common deductions. These are donations to Goodwill or religious offerings. For your charitable contribution to be recognized as a deduction, however, you must list your tax credits, which is called itemizing your deductions.

If your itemized deductions do not add up to more than the standard deduction, it doesn't benefit you to itemize.

Keep in mind that certain life events can affect your taxes. If you got married or divorced, started supporting your parents or sibling, or even had a child, your tax bracket can change. Be sure to re-evaluate your taxes and withholdings when these life events happen.

I can nerd out even more about this, but I won't do it here. I think I've overwhelmed you already with charts and figures. If you are interested in more charts, you can find it in the Bonus Nerd Stuff chapter.

This chapter was to simply introduce you to taxes. There are some many more things that I don't know and goes outside of the bounds of this book. These tax basics should give you enough to file taxes for the first few years. I encourage you to look deeper into ways to proper file your taxes.

15

401k

When you get your first "real" job, you are going to get bombarded with all these decisions that you never had to make before. One of the most important ones will be about a 401(k).

What is a 401K?

A 401(k) is a standard type of retirement plan. Essentially, you take a percentage (or specific amount) of money from your check every pay period to go towards your retirement. This money is taken out "before taxes."

I've heard of this phrase before, but what does that mean?

When money is taken out "before taxes," this means that you can lower your taxable income, which helps to change which tax bracket you're in. Essentially, lowering how much taxes you owe.[57]

---

[57] See the chapter on Taxes

What should I know before money is taken out of my check?

Look through all that benefit paperwork and find out if your company matches your contribution, and how long you must be vested.

What the what?

The amount you invest into your 401(k) is your contribution. Most companies will match the amount of money that you put in your 401(k), but only up to a certain percentage of your salary. The amount I've most commonly seen is 3 percent. Sometimes they'll word it, "100 percent match, up to 3 percent" or "50 percent match, up to 6 percent." My recommendation is you at least contribute the amount your company is willing to match. If they are matching up to 3 percent, then you should invest at least 3 percent.

You may hear that you need to be "vested" in the company for X amount of years. Vesting means ownership. To be fully vested, means that you own 100% of the amount contributed by your company. Companies like to ensure you are invested in the company and this gives an incentive for you to stay with them. That percentage increases the longer you stay with a company.

Example: Your company policy states it will match 5 percent of your contributions; fully vested after four years.

Years	Percent Vested
1	25%
2	50%
3	75%
4	100%

Imagine your salary is $100K. If you contribute 10 percent of your salary to your 401(k), then you will contribute a total of $10K each year. Your company will only match 5 percent of how much you put in, so they will put in $500 (5% of $10,000). By the end of year, you will have $10,500 in your 401(k).

Sweet, right? Not so much. Four years vested means that you will not get all of that $500 until you've been with the company for four years. Not calendar years. Anniversary years. Every year you stay with the company, the more you get contributed to your retirement. The chart below shows your contributions to your 401(k) between what you invest and what your company invests per year.

Years Vested	Your contribution	Company's Contribution (Yearly)	% Vested	Company's Actual Contrib.	If you leave this year
1	$10000	$500	25%	$125	$10,125
2	$10000	$500	50%	$250	$20,250
3	$10000	$500	75%	$750	$30,750
4	$10000	$500	100%	$500	$40,500
5	$10000	$500	100%	$500	$60,000

Ok I have matched my company's contribution. Now, what do I do now?

Now you need to pick the best stocks and mutual funds.

What?! I thought we were talking about 401(k)s.

We still are. A company that offers a 401(k) plan typically offers employees a choice of several investment options. The employee can choose one or several funds to invest in. Most of the options are mutual funds, and they may include index funds, large-cap and small-cap funds, foreign funds, real estate funds, and bond funds. I'm sure I've lost you by now. That's exactly how it feels when you get a 401(k) and no one explains any of this to you. While the totality of what all this means is beyond the scope of this book, the main advice I can give for younger folks is to mix it up with conservative, aggressive stocks, and mutual funds. A lot of the larger investment companies offer a financial manager that will answer any questions you have but they will not give you financial advice. These advisors can be liable if they give you very specific advice about your portfolio. Due to this, they are simply there to give you general information about investing. They will let you know things like how being a younger investor, you have a little bit more flexibility to take risks in the market. For the person that isn't that interested, this will not mean shit to you until you leave your company.

What do I do when I leave my company?

When you leave your company, you need to take your money out of your company's 401(k). Key things to note: 1) they charge you a fee if you keep your money in the account without being attached to a company; 2) if you join a new company, you need to rollover your 401(k) into your new plan.

Rollover? Like old school T-Mobile minutes?

Uh...yea...sure. It's just a fancy term for transfer. Now when you get the form to transfer your money, it will give you an option to take 100 percent of the money out and keep it yourself. **Don't do this!** It is taxed about 20 percent and you will have to start your retirement fund all over again. By rolling it over to another account, you don't have to worry about any fees or taxes. Oftentimes, they will mail you the check, and you have to mail it to your new provider.

There are several other ways to save for retirement. If you are with the government, they have a similar plan called Thrift Savings Plan (TSP) that will give you easier options to invest. The L Fund, Lifecycle Fund, is a managed investment option where they use professionally determined investment strategies that are tailored to meet your goals.

The information here can still assist you with managing your basic investment accounts. I've laid the foundation. Now when you go off and research more, you aren't going in 100 percent blind.

16 stocks

One day my stepfather told me, "I made $16 in my sleep." At first, I thought, *he's a crazy old man,* but the more I talked to him about it the less crazy he sounded. Essentially, what he was saying is that his money was making money. He did no work; literally was asleep. Yet, he managed to make $16! What if you made $16 every time you went to sleep? That's the goal. To have your money work for you; have your money making money. That's when I started to look into stocks. I'd heard that I need to *diversify* my money. I had no idea what that meant. This was another field that I thought only wealthy people participated in. What I managed to piece together is that it's basically a simple concept that you may have heard, *don't put all your eggs in one basket.* This isn't something that just applies to your finances but many aspects of life. You shouldn't concentrate all your resources to one area, you could lose it all. You want to spread out your resources to take advantage of multiple opportunities. You take a large gamble by doing that. Think of it as spending all your savings on one lottery ticket. Absurd!

With all that said, the stock market is definitely not something that you just *jump* into. It's the equivalent of deciding to work out, so you do a triathlon. There are many aspects to the stock market, and they should all be thoroughly researched before you actually start using real money. I've found a myriad of websites that allow you to "play" around before you commit. Here are a few suggestions: Google Finance, OptionsHouse, and Wall Street Survivor. Wall Street Survivor and OptionsHouse are also great resources to learn the lingo. A great first lesson to learn about the stock market is there aren't just stocks. There are mutual funds, bonds, and more that you can learn about from the aforementioned websites. And within stocks, there are a variety of types— international, penny, etc. Hopefully you can start to see why diving into the stock market isn't to be taken lightly. Within any category there could be three or four more subcategories. Complete a thorough research on any topic before using real money. This chapter should be used simply to get a general understanding of the stock market.

shares

You can have stock in a company. Stock is a collection of "shares." A share is a piece of ownership. By the transitive property, by buying stock in a company you own a piece of that company. Imagine if the company was a pie, and it was cut into several small pieces. By buying stock, you are buying one of the small pieces of the pie, which now makes you an owner of the pie. If you own enough of the pie, you determine what happens to the pie.

trades

To buy stock, it is called trading. But beware! You can't go buying stocks all willy-nilly! Most companies charge you a fee for every transaction you make. I've seen the fees go up to $10.95 per transaction. I'm sure there are places that have transaction fees that are more than that. You can probably find companies that don't charge a fee. I suggest you look into how the company intends to make a profit if not off trade fees. I use a great app called Robinhood. It doesn't charge you any transaction fees. They make their money off the interest of your money stored in their account.

the • quick • & • dirty • about • stocks

Recently, I had to explain stocks to my friends, here is how I explained stocks:

Say there is a company called I Don't Know Industries (IDK) and that the stock has plummeted from fifty to twenty dollars. You recently learned that you should "Sell High and Buy Low" (umm...ok...sure). That means if the stock price is high, you should sell. However, if it's low you should buy. Sounds backwards, but it works.

You have $100 and decided that you will buy five shares of IDK for $20 dollars, and you now own five shares of the company, IDK. Your shares are currently worth twenty dollars each. If you sell them immediately (and nothing has changed in the market), they will be still worth twenty dollars each. But if you wait for the shares to increase in value, say back to fifty dollars each, you are now $150 richer! The math is explained below:

$$Profit\ per\ share\ =\ New\ Price\ -\ Purchase\ Price$$
$$Profit\ per\ share\ =\ \$50\ -\ \$20$$
$$Profit\ per\ share\ =\ \$30$$
$$Total\ Profit\ =\ Number\ of\ shares\ \times\ Profit\ per\ share$$
$$Total\ Profit\ =\ 5\ shares\ \times\ \$30$$
$$Total\ Profit\ =\ \$150$$

Now imagine if the stock fluctuates and went down to ten dollars. Now your twenty-dollar stock is worth half the amount.

$$Profit\ per\ share\ =\ New\ Price\ -\ Purchase\ Price$$
$$Profit\ per\ share\ =\ \$10\ -\ \$20$$
$$Profit\ per\ share\ =\ -\$10$$
$$Total\ Loss\ =\ Number\ of\ shares\ \times\ Profit\ per\ share$$
$$Total\ Loss\ =\ 5\ shares\ \times\ -\$10$$
$$Total\ Loss\ =\ -\$50$$

You could do a few things at this point:

- Sell: if you think that this stock isn't going to do any better any time soon, then you should sell.
- Wait: wait to see if the stock will go up. Sometimes when it drops, people see that it's cheaper, buy a shitload, and your stock price skyrockets.

- Buy more: What the what!? Why in the world would I buy more stock if this shit is plummeting? Because now you can get the stock at a cheaper price, and if it goes back up, you can make mo' money.
- Set a stop limit: This is advanced shit right here. Master the first three methods first before trying this.

i p o s

When a company decides to put its company on the stock market, they offer an Initial Public Offering (IPO) to the public. This is hopefully the lowest the stock will ever be. Getting in on the ground floor requires two things: hope and research.

You should **research** exactly how the company has been doing prior to the IPO and find out what their plans are for the future. If it sounds like something that you can get behind, then you should consider that company.

You **hope** that the company will do well. Buying IPOs are the ultimate risk because there is no stock market history to go by, and just because it did well before doesn't necessarily mean it will do well moving forward.

s t o c k • q u e s t i o n s

Here are some questions that my friends had, and the answers I gave:

- How do you buy stocks?

   You have to set up an account with your trading company. It typically takes about 3-7 days to transfer money into your account. You can't use credit. You must transfer money from your bank account. It's not linked to your bank account, so they aren't going to just pull money from your account. You tell them how much you want them to pull out and they will in a one-time transaction, just like if you were to transfer money to someone's bank account.

- Why do they need my social security number?

   Tax purposes. Stocks are taxed at the end of the year. You are taxed on any stocks that you cash out.

- How do I add stock?

   You need to identify the stock symbol associated with the stock you want to purchase. The stock symbol is typically 1-5 letters. Example: F (Ford); GE (General Electric); JCP (JCPenny); TWTR (Twitter). From there, you follow the steps within your trading service.

- When is the market open?

   The New York Stock Exchange (NYSE) market hours are from Monday – Friday, 9:30 a.m. to 4:00 p.m. EST.

- Is the market open on holidays?

The market is closed on the following holidays: New Year's Day, Martin Luther King, Jr. Observance Day, President's Day, Good Friday, Memorial Day, Independence Day, Labor Day, Thanksgiving, and Christmas.

- Can I buy stock after hours?

   Yes, but you will purchase it at whatever price the market opens at.

- What? Why isn't it the same price as when it closes?

   There are extended hours. Typically, this is an additional service that you have to pay for. The hours are 4-9:30 a.m. and 4-6:30 p.m. The market still goes on as normal, so the price of the stock you want may increase or decrease overnight.

- Why doesn't the description of this stock match what I thought it was?

   For example, there are plenty of marijuana stocks. But you wouldn't know if you didn't look it up. They want to make sure the million and billionaires don't get looked at crazy when their accountants see they have $10K in WEED.

- How many shares should I buy?

   That all depends on how much you are willing to spend. Each company's stock price is different, so buying ten shares of TWTR is significantly less money than buying ten shares of APPL.

- When should I sell?

    That's up to you. No one will ever tell you explicitly that you should buy or sell. It takes research and understanding the market to make that determination. Getting more tips is beyond the scope of this book. However, I do suggest that you dive deeper into this.

- If I drop down to the negative, will I owe money?

    There is no way to go in the negative. You can only get to zero.

- Is my beginning share price locked in or will I have to pay the new price?

    If you buy a share on Tuesday, and then determine you want more on Thursday, you will have to pay the new price.

- When I sell shares, I'm selling to other people?

    Meh. Think of it as if you are selling it back to the pool of available shares. Someone else can then buy your shares at a totally different price than when you bought them.

sh!t labor

You must do something you've never done to get something you've never had.

While I have you here, I figure I should touch on a topic that some of you may have read in other books. I'm talking about being a woman in the workplace. I have read my fair share of awesome books on the topic, but I feel like some of the books have left out some key things that apply to women like me: a minority engineer. I've grown to learn that I'm very much a unicorn. People have heard of minority female engineers, but not many have seen one out in the wild. Yet here I am, just as real as you are.

Every aspect of being a minority female engineer comes with its own set of injustices. The most convenient way to discuss this is to break it down into sections. Even if you've come upon this chapter and aren't female, nor minority, nor an engineer, you still can gain some nuggets of wisdom. Even if it's just a better understanding of what it means to be a unicorn.

17

a minority

As a minority female, my presence typically stops the majority of folk from saying things that they otherwise would have said. They start becoming acutely aware of the racist or sexist things they normally say. However, if you stay anywhere long enough, every now and then someone's true colors show through. Their box they've put you and your people in will become clear.

An unexpected outcome of being the minority in the office is when they learn you are "one of the cool ones." You are then expected to become the resident go-to for *all* diversity questions. Once you open the door to allow for a single race-related question, you become the Diversity Captain. You now must answer all the questions that they've ever had about your race or gender. Speaking from the viewpoint of someone who has been the African American Diversity Captain many times, some of the first questions I've received are about hair. It has never failed. Whether they've gotten comfortable enough to offer to help braid your hair in the bathroom[58] or ask you the cost of weave; the hair questions will never cease to exist.

The price of weave is probably the most asked question I've received. Seeing as I have never bought a weave, I make shit up because they won't stop at "I don't know." My go-to response is, "Well it depends. [take an obligatory pause] There's two parts to it: the hair and the service to get it installed. [insert collective gasp and whispered confusion, "installed?"] Hair can cost anywhere between two and four hundred dollars a bundle. You'll need about two to four bundles depending on how much hair you have. Then, installation is no less than $200." If you are a weave-wearing connoisseur, then you already know I'm making it all up. They don't know...shit! And neither do I. Don't assume every Black woman knows about everything Black hair. I honestly can't tell you if someone's hair is real or fake, or if it's a lace front or a wig. I'm still trying to figure out how they get their hair under a wig. In all honesty, I should refer them to a YouTube video. That's where I get my information.

The assumption that all people know all things about their culture is quite annoying.[59] There are Black folks brushing up on their Black trivia every night. Every minority has a different story from the narrative that is portrayed in the media, whether it's in television programs, news, or social media. These tales lead the majority to fit you in that box which you find yourself constantly trying to kick your way out.

---

[58] True story. Definitely matrix'ed my way out of that situation.

[59] I can only speak from the Black perspective.

A form of microaggression that you can expect comes in the form of those seemingly innocent questions. These subtle issues happen regularly but are so minute that they can get overlooked.

When I was working with this one company in DC, I found myself in an unorthodox environment. I was a minority, yet in a way I'd never been before. I was the only Black woman around a majority of Indians. There were three white dudes, and two Ethiopian guys. We all grew to be a weird little family.

One day, John[60], one of the white guys, decided he wanted to ask everyone where they lived. Seemingly innocent question. right? I walked in his view and when he asked me, I stated Alexandria. He remarked, "Oh, I thought you lived in Anacostia." I just walked away. Now, for those who are unaware, at the time of this writing Anacostia is what the DC locals call Southeast, meaning Southeast DC. Its demographics[61] are 5 percent white, 3 percent other, and can you guess what the other 92 percent? That's right, Black. John got the muthafuckin' side eye. Now, this sort of microaggression often gets written off as a "one-time thing" by others and sometimes it is just that. However, when 'one time' becomes 'all the time,' you start to paint the picture.

As an employed minority, you must constantly deal with John-like shit every day. Try to resist punching John square in his jaw because your bank account requires you to be employed. Typically, addressing the individual head on about the issue will help to reduce the number of

---

[60] That's not his name.
[61] According to the 2000 U.S. Census

incidents you have. Most people don't like the perception of having racist tendency so they will go out of their way to ensure that they don't offend you. Some may take it overboard to "prove a point." Such as asking if its ok if they say a statement or overly checking in. Some may consider you a threat to *their* employment and will restrain from interacting with you altogether.

Recently, I had to confront a co-worker about some racist remarks she'd made to me about other co-workers. After first I thought it was a one-time occurrence and decided not to rock the boat. Something I think we all do. We just hope that they don't do it again, so we don't have to confront them. We fear the unknown. We don't know if confront them if will send the other individual in a tizzy or if it will affect the working relationship. The last thing anyone wants is to make life difficult for themselves in the workplace.

However, she started to do it more often. I realized my mistake was not nipping it in the bud in the beginning. By allowing her to open the door with the first remarks, I was essentially telling her that we were like-minded, and she should continue. I reached out to her to let her know that I support inclusion and wasn't comfortable with the types of comments she was making. She apologized and hasn't made any off-color comments since! Our relationship wasn't affected by it and I appreciate her more now! This could have gone completely different. However, it shows the maturity of my co-worker and that even at mid-career there are still some things that we can all learn.

18

a minority female

I went to a predominantly Black elementary school, high school, college, and graduate school. I didn't experience culture shock until I went to a conference in graduate school. I was at the Optical Fiber Communication Conference in Anaheim, California, way back in 2006.

I walked in with my fellow minority folk and was instantly shocked to submission. It was the first time I'd been in a room where I could count the African Americans and women, [62]and that's exactly what I did. I made a point to see how many people attending the conference were African American and how many people were women. The only people that fit both of the categories were me and my advisor! I was so intimidated. I'd never been around so many old, white men in my entire life.

---

[62] Which were not mutually inclusive.

Being a minority woman puts you in a very small box. There's an old adage that says, "You must work twice as hard to get half as far." This is a phrase that most minorities have heard. Yet for minority women, we must work twice as hard to get a quarter as far. We bust our asses to make sure that the things we do don't reflect poorly on our race or gender. We have to scrutinize everything we say, feel or write, simply because we are making sure that we don't make it worse for the next one who follows us. We don't want them to think they can't hire another Latina because the last one was too feisty, or another African American woman because the previous one got labelled the Angry Black Woman when some idiot couldn't do his fucking job. You can't just go over and say, "Steve, what the fuck, yo?!" You'll get, "Hey, Nina! Calm down." I'd rather you stab me in my ocular lens than tell to calm me to down. That's a guaranteed way to get a woman upset. Yet, we must hold our composure or fear being labelled the office bitch. We must endure guys talking over us, repeating what we say, or straight up ignoring the words that come out. There are some fantastic books out there about being a woman in the workplace.[63] I have experienced everything I just named.[64] Being a woman and minority in the workplace requires a level of confidence, strong will, and attitude.

I was changed when I heard Mindy Kaling as Mindy Lahiri say, "Lord, give me the confidence of a mediocre white man." Mindy gained much backlash for this statement. For me it offered me a new look on life. I started to truly carry myself as if I were a mediocre white man in the

---

[63] "Lean In" by Sheryl Sandberg holds up to the hype.

[64] Even being told by 2 guys at the same time to calm down.

workplace. I walked into rooms as if I were entitled to have all the same things my counterparts (who were mostly white males) would have. I sat at the head of tables as if I were conducting the meeting. I made sure that I was known in the office, and that this Black woman had as much right to be in the conversation as anyone else in the room. The only difference between me and a mediocre white man is that I knew my shit! I received a lot of strange looks from some. However, the overall response was as respect. It was strange to command unearned respect from people, but it allowed me to get my job done in a more streamline fashion. I stop having to wait my turn to speak or tell people that it was my meeting so I'm running it. Getting met with a headstrong woman confuses some. There are those people that like to pontificate. Usually these individuals are what I like to call *loud and wrong* because they like to talk over people and just spatter out the first thing they can think on that topic. Letting them have their day in the sun is important for them. I acknowledge them with, "Thanks for that Ryan but today we're discussing..." That lets them know I heard you, but also you are wrong. I also found that giving the blank stare and double blink works as well. As if to say, I have no words for that.

I make sure that I don't take on any stereotypical female role. Although I usually like my co-workers and I enjoy planning things, I made a conscious decision not to plan any birthday parties or office events. I'm not the one that goes out to get a birthday card to pass around. I found that once you do it, they will make some bullshit ass excuse that you should always do it. I felt like the office manager. I was the go-to for going away events or birthdays or holiday parties. In the beginning, I was honored that the team though I was so great at hosting. However, after the fifth or sixth time, I realized that they were pigeon-holing me into a position I'd rallied against my whole life, the stereotypical secretary. Now, I refuse participate any more than signing a card or showing up. In conjunction with that, I do not volunteer to take meeting minutes. I don't want to be preoccupied with keeping the minutes that I can't contribute to the conversation.

Sometimes you must decide whether you are a woman or a minority first. Hardly will you be able to make a blanket declaration as to which comes first. Rarely do people think of minority women when they think women. I recently experienced this in a women's group. I noticed that a lot of the events were very majority based, so I voiced how I'd like to do more events specifically for women of color. I received one of the highest reactions to a message in the group. Have we had an event specifically for women of color? Nope. It's very controversial to speak on race, so the best thing is to avoid it in mixed company. That's why we watched the film *Betty White: First Lady of Television* instead of *He Named Me Malala* for a group event. Because Betty White is the best thing **before** sliced bread[65], she's a safe choice. Malala doesn't spark universal joy like Betty. It's times like these where you feel like you can't win as a minority woman. Should you simply be satisfied that we are paying attention to women, or should you be offended that being a woman means you can't also be Black or Asian or Latina? From my experience, navigating who you identify as never gets easier. You just learn to pick your battles.

---

[65] Apparently, she was born in 1922. This is before sliced bread was invented, which was in 1928.

19

a minority female engineer

Being a minority female engineer checks a lot of boxes. It also is quite a lonely place. Being an engineer is already a restrictive field, but a woman in the field is like a unicorn. When you throw minority in the mix, you are now the rarest Patronus there is.[66] I am habitually the only woman on the team. At the time of this writing, I have never worked with another woman on my team with the same position as me.[67] It's not shocking if I hear that one of the guys on my team (or all) has never worked with a woman. On top of that, it's even unlikelier that they've worked with a minority female engineer, and that just brings up more that can go wrong.

Whenever I start a new job, I must prove myself all over again. Understandably, whenever anyone joins a new team, they must prove themselves on some level. As a woman, there is an eextra level that you

---

[66] What up, Harry Potter reference!

[67] I've worked with women, but they are typically in a Project Manager role so something similar.

must conquer to prove yourself. Everyone sees you as a damsel in distress. In the beginning of my career, I would get offended by it. I knew my shit. What the fuck, bro? Now, I just see it as part of the hazing process. Just a form of initiation. You have to get past it. What I found to be quite helpful in speeding up the process and to cut them off when they start to mansplain something to you. Ensuring that you are using the proper jargon, so you don't have to endure someone dumbing it down for you. To play devil's advocate, since there aren't many female engineers most of the women the male engineers encounter may not be technical. Therefore, they must simplify it. To use the correct terminology is the gateway to showing that you are a true engineer. Some guys will be taken aback however, they'll acknowledge you know what's going on and proceed to treat you like a peer. Others will keep talking as if you didn't say a word. Which brings me to my next point: picking your battles.

I am a feminist at heart. You and I know that there is no such thing as a perfect feminist. We can't fight every battle. We'd be drained. Especially if you fought every battle in the workplace, then you'd have little time to actually do your job. That's why in the workplace you need to decide which battles you are willing to fight.

The battle I have decided to fight is sexist comments. I once had a co-worker say to me, "We are supposed to get another female on the team. I'm cool as long as your thangs don't sync up. I can't have two people yelling for no reason." Article I, Section 2 of the type of shit I'm not dealing with today. Bitch, what did you say to me! That's something you just shouldn't say in life, let alone at work! I confronted him in front of the team about this comment. This was important because I wanted everyone to see that I'm not "one of the boys" and there is a line that they can't cross. He tried to pass it off as, "Forgive me, for I have never worked with someone with lady parts." Dude! Seriously, that's your rebuttal? It doesn't matter if I have lady parts, male parts, or no parts! Don't say shit like that...EVER!

Here is another example where I had to decide if the battle to fight. By way of pure seniority, I ended up becoming the team lead of a project. On this project, I was the Subject Matter Expert (SME), which meant no one knew more than I did.[68]

There was an intense learning curve, but it was doable. It had taken me about six months to conquer the software that I'd installed and configured. That was six months of me teaching myself everything about the software. All the male engineers that came on board the team were able to ask me any questions they had. Their learning curve was reduced by half.[69] My team grew big enough that we were moved to our own office space. It was an open office concept. There were no cubicles just desks and computers.

Midway through the project, we got a new team member; let's call him Kevin. Kevin had never used the software we were using, yet he refused to believe that he would have the same learning curve as his teammates.

---

[68] Facts: I didn't know that much but I knew more than everyone else. More about this in Titles

[69] It is not lost on me that I literally did, twice as much to get the same

One day, my business analyst and I were working on the project schedule and discussed how Kevin should probably work with a senior engineer to complete a portion of the schedule. Since it was an open office, Kevin overheard. He insisted that he could take on the entire portion on his own. Knowing this wasn't possible, I explained that I didn't doubt his mental capacity to complete the task and explained that due to the high learning curve it would be pretty difficult for him to make the deadline. At this revelation, he proceeded to *yell* his demands at me in front of my entire team. Internally, I was thinking, "Who in the fuck are you yelling at?! The fuck!? You *just* got here. You don't know shit! You betta be lucky I need this fucking job." Instead, I gave a blank stare and double blinked all while my entire team stared at me. I took a deep breath and explained to him that he must meet the deadline by any means necessary. End of conversation. As I predicted, Kevin had problems with the learning curve. He would blatantly go to all the other members on the team, and when they all responded with, "I don't know how, but Erica does," he refused to ask me for help. Again, as I predicted, Kevin didn't meet his deadline and went to my supervisor to blame me for not helping him. By this time, my supervisor was well aware of my work ethic and knew that Kevin was cray cray. Kevin ended up getting reprimanded.

I always wondered if Kevin would have lashed out as he did if I was a man. Maybe he would have, but in my experience, there are a lot of men who feel they can speak to women any way they please. And in fear that any semblance of annoyance or anger or passion can turn me into the Angry Black Woman or accused of being on my period, I bite my lip and don't say anything. As women, we maintain this illusion that we are calm and collected, when in actuality we are pissed off and mad.

Being a woman in a male dominated profession requires a high tolerance of ignorant shit and knowing when to fight.

Boys will be boys.

As controversial as that statement can get, generally it's true. They mostly like to laugh at the stupidest things. When you are around a guy, albeit, your brother, boyfriend, or husband, there will be some silly things that will happen that only they find absolutely hilarious. Now imagine a whole team of that. I've learned to adapt. Most of the things are innocent, *that's what she said* jokes, farting and belching. Maybe there will be unexplained reasons why they refuse to wash their oatmeal bowl but continue to eat out of it every morning.[70] These are swords I've chosen not to fall on. I'm not personally offend and if they do cross the line, which is rare, I'll address it. They tend to know my limits and play well within them.

---

[70] I recognize that that's oddly specific.

20

knowing your environment

A friend, Brianna, and I were having a general conversation about our professions, and how we interact with the people that we work with. Just to give you some context, she holds a management position in the military and, as you know, I'm an IT consultant. We both fight the constant battle of being a Black female in a male-dominated field. However, there are many things that we do completely different. It was extremely baffling to each of us why the other would behave in that manner. What we came to understand is that we have learned to adjust to our unique environments. All people, male, female, or non-conforming binary, learn to adjust to their environment. We all have boundaries we will not cross and some that just goes with the environment.

For instance, I'd started my new position as a SharePoint Engineer in Washington D.C. where I worked in a very professional building. I walked into a crowd of people in the front with business suits. I was lucky that I had a friend that I'd worked with at a prior job, so I wasn't there alone. On the second day, in the office, I was innocently filling out standard onboarding paperwork when suddenly, there was a full-on Nerf gun war! I was used as a human shield. It was NUTS! I'd never worked in an environment where we could have fun in the office! That same day I logged onto Amazon and purchased a six-shooter to join the war two days later.[71] I was excited I was working in an environment that was so relaxed.

When I told my friend this, she gave me a blank stare. I thought maybe she didn't hear me. I repeated it with the same, if not more, enthusiasm! I was met once again with a blank stare. I yelled, "Who wouldn't want to work somewhere where you have Nerf gun battles!?" She looked at me with all seriousness and said, "I think that's cool, but if I worked there, I wouldn't participate." I was immediately taken aback. I thought maybe she thought it was just too close to my hire date for me to become so relaxed. I asked why she wouldn't. She said, "I don't know. I just don't think that you should be doing that at work." I was still perplexed. Why wouldn't you want to have fun at work? You spend one-third of your day at work, why wouldn't you want to enjoy it? But what I wasn't considering was what environment she was used to. Coming from a military angle, she saw it as laziness. Not doing your job. You are being paid to work and spending a portion of your paid workday shooting Nerf guns was a waste of time. I agreed with that if I looked at it from a managerial perspective. But as a worker bee, I saw it as camaraderie.

---

[71] #AmazonPrime

Activities like this helped us to not only relax given such a stressful position we had, but it also allowed us to bond as a team. That bond allowed us to work better together.

At my job, the work was tough, and the days were long and exhausting. You could burn out if you worked all day. In some states, it is legally required that you take breaks. At my workplace, our supervisor allowed for our five minutes of play time since he trusted that we would get our work done on time and accurately. What he trusted about the team was that we knew when to work and when to play. We would drop anything if something needed attention. We didn't let our play affect our performance. Also, we looked at it like a smoke break. None of us actually smoked. Smoking a cigarette takes approximately seven minutes. If you have to leave the building, that smoke break could last up to fifteen minutes. Bathroom breaks are the same way. I can make my argument all day. I know it wouldn't change my friend's mind because she's never worked in the type of environments I have. Her position is governed by a massive set of federal rules, and in her mind, playing Nerf gun wars was not professional.

Throughout my years of work, however, I've learned that no one really tells you what is "professional." You learn through trial and error and observation, and for each place you work at, the definition of professional varies. Each environment promotes a different type of professionalism; some, like my Nerf gun workplace, are slightly more relax, but still professional. For my friend's job, professional meant something else. The key to figuring it out for both of us was to be aware of our environment and know that we were conforming to it. While maintaining our workplace's unique style of professionalism, we were able to assert ourselves to display our hard work and integrity.

21

surround yourself

A couple of months ago, my co-worker and friend, José, and I went out for lunch, as we did every day. We talked about everything: life, finances, and relationships. This particular lunch he decided to tell me how his girlfriend had decided to go for a higher position in her company. Until she'd met him, she'd was not motivated to seek a higher position. He couldn't understand why she didn't try to ask for more before. From the conversations he'd had with her, she knew was doing much more than her position required. However, she was ok with making a third of his pay and he didn't know why. I explained how there are a couple of factors at play here. The first is having the courage to say, I deserve more and go after it. As women, we feel we need to be absolutely perfect before asking for what we want. We dissect job descriptions until we convince ourselves that we aren't qualified for the position.

The second is not having the right circle of people around you. What José didn't recognize is that his girlfriend never had anyone tell her that she could and should strive for more. She didn't realize that she was lacking until she met him.

I explained to José that his girlfriend didn't strive for more because she didn't know that she should be asking for more. She thought that she should be satisfied what was being given to her. She thought that if they wanted her to have more, they would give it to her. By dating him, she started to learn that she needed to find courage to ask for her worth. He said he had no idea that females were less confident and that I should write a book.[72]

The old saying, "Surround yourself with like-minded people," is great advice. I would go even further to say, "Surround yourself with people you want to become."[73] To tell you the truth, I'm pretty sure my dad told me this before, but I didn't know what he was talking about.[74] It just seemed like an odd concept, especially because I didn't know who I wanted to become.

Luckily, I was exposed to this concept before I could put a name to it. Back in the eighties, the Portsmouth Public School system grouped students according to their academic abilities. Portsmouth decided to surround me with like-minded people. My family had moved to Chesapeake for my second-grade schooling, but by the next year we were

---

[72] He will definitely take credit for this book, but the truth is, I started this book longer before that conversation. But that's not going to stop him telling everyone it was all his idea.

[73] I'm pretty sure this isn't a new quote

[74] Probably because I was 6 and didn't understand any of his heart-to-hearts

back in Portsmouth. Since I was just rejoining the system late, they just placed me in a class that had space and I wound up in Mrs. Hubbard's third grade class. It was an alright class. Nothing too spectacular. You know, just third graders doing third grade things. However, it didn't take long for me to learn that Mrs. Wright's class existed. Mrs. Wright's class was structured to challenge each student. The students were specifically chosen for her class because of the intellectual talents they had. I knew in my heart that I belonged in her class and not in Mrs. Hubbard's.[75] To be honest, the only things I remember from Mrs. Hubbard's class is how to write in cursive, how she kept us quiet by having us write each number from one to 10,000, and how I forgot to spell "who" after a trip to Jamestown. My third-grade memories are mostly composed of yearning to be in Mrs. Wright's class.

I tried everything to get in her class, to no avail. Luckily, there was a special session called the Gifted and Talented class. This class was designed for the brightest kids in that grade to meet weekly for an hour to learn more challenging shit. We did projects on international relations, were exposed to advanced math concepts and given reading assignments that were a grade or two higher in difficulty. I was identified as gifted and so was **most** of Mrs. Wright's class. It was during this session where I finally felt challenged. This further proved to me that I belonged in Mrs. Wright's class, but as much as I kicked and screamed, I was never transferred. However, the next year I was placed in the "smart" class.

---

[75] No shade to Mrs. Hubbard.

From that point until the end of *secondary education*, I had class with the same group of people. Yes, that's right! From fourth grade until twelfth, I looked at the same twelve to fifteen faces. If anyone was in the class we didn't recognize, we all knew they were either in the wrong class and would be gone soon, or that it was a new kid and we need to size them up. By 'size them up,' I mean mentally. We were a class full of nerds.[76]

Since the school system had this regime in place, I was encouraged to go to college. While I got into all the schools I applied to, I attended the school that offer a program that focused on science, technology, engineering, and mathematics (STEM) majors. Originally, the program was called Dozoretz National Institute for Minorities in Applied Sciences (DNIMAS) for students that looked like me and had the same goals and drive.[77] I am still extremely close with many of the people I met in the program. Throughout the years, we've learned how to grow together. Going through a lot of the same stages in life, we were able to bounce ideas off of each other and call on each other for help.

Have you ever found yourself adopting a phrase that a friend says all the time? That's because we subconsciously absorb things that we get from our surroundings. Imagine if the things that you absorbed were positive points to help you become a better more successful person. That's why the people you surround yourself with is important. You grow as large as your circle. Keep people around you who inspire you to do

---

[76] But we were cool...I swear!...well not me but a lot of them were. The class valedictorian was also the prom queen.

[77] Shout out to Norfolk State University's DNIMAS program!! #D-Unit

better things. If you don't have the privilege of having made lifelong friends through a systematic regime, finding those people may require you a little leg work. You may want to start going to events that spark your interest or join a club that has the type of people that you want to associate with.

Sometimes, the people I want to become may have a personality trait that I am attracted to, and I strive to emulate that. People that have different goals and aspirations can help motivate you to complete or start a goal. I have a lot of friends that have goals that I am not interested in, but their dedication inspires me to give the same amount of dedication to completing a goal I have.

We typically keep connected with each other in some sort of group chat. When we are looking for answers we reach out because someone will either know the answer or can point us in the right direction. We use each other as resources.

If you find that either you or the people within your circle are jealous of each other's accomplishments, you may want to look a little deeper into that relationship. If you find that you are the one that is jealous when others tell you about their accomplishments, try to understand what it is about their success that you want. Do you want the attention? Do you want the prestige? It becomes a deeper conversation. If you find that the people in your circle aren't as encouraging, maybe you need a new circle to give you a different perspective.

At a certain point, if you are doing it right, you will transition to become the point of inspiration, the desired person to want to be around. You will start acquiring knowledge that others will want, or you will radiate an air that will move people to gravitate around you. It will be your obligation to continue the cycle, to give that person the same motivation given to you to become successful. This is how mentorships are born.

22

titles

Throughout your career you will encounter many titles. Titles that describe a position you are seeking. Titles that you have to answer to. Titles that you will receive. Oftentimes, these titles are intimidating, especially to recent graduates trying to get their foot in the door. We get caught up in titles and suspect that we don't meet the job description. This is a major reason why women don't apply for certain jobs. We believe that they aren't a **[insert any job title here],** so we can't do that job. We feel if we don't fit every single one of the bullets, then we aren't suited for the job. Here's a secret: most of the guys that apply for jobs don't know anything either.

When I became a Nuclear Engineer, I realized that titles are just words. An elaborate pairing of words to make what you do sound fancy. Yes, a Nuclear Engineer sounds badass as hell; however, I was only labeled 'Nuclear' because the work I did involve a nuclear machine. I didn't actually do anything with the nuclear part of it. Matter of fact, I created spreadsheets. **Yes, spreadsheets!** Yet they called me a Nuclear Engineer.

I made spreadsheets about a nuclear machine, and I got to pose as a badass. When people asked me what I did for a living, I proudly said, "Nuclear Engineer," knowing no one would ask more than that. When people heard "Nuclear Engineer," that translated to "Rocket Scientist," which automatically made me a smart motherfucker. I knew, though, I just made spreadsheets. The people I worked with knew I made spreadsheets. Fuckin' EXCEL SPREADSHEETS! I should have been called Excel Expert. Nope! You couldn't even call me that! I didn't know that much about Excel. So, it was more like Excel Power User. Yes, I know a little more than a normal person, but I still don't know what PivotTables are.

Since being a Nuclear Engineer, I've had the honor of being labeled several things: SharePoint Developer, SharePoint Administrator, K2 Subject Matter Expert, Senior SharePoint Engineer, and Cloud Architect. All those titles may sound fancy, but to me they are just words. I was a Subject Matter Expert (SME)[78] simply because I knew more on that subject than anyone else that worked there. Let me give you an example: if I asked you to find out if Oreos make Pumpkin Spice Oreos, you will have to go do a little research. Eventually, you find out they do make them (really?!). You are now the SME of Oreos. Yes, that is literally how I became the SME of K2. At the time, I didn't feel like the SME. I was aware that I knew more than everyone, but Subject Matter Expert sounds a bit

---

[78] Pronounced smee

aggressive. Subject Matter Expert to me sounded as if I knew every single thing there was to know about the subject, and that simply was not true.

Around the same time, I was named a SME, I learned that the people with "impressive" titles were rarely impressive. There were several people I've met that were labeled SME or Senior and knew less than I did. We would have a conversation with a customer, and they would say something that I knew to be false. At first, I thought it was just a slip up. I started to doubt myself because certainly this SME knew more than me. However, the longer they'd speak the more I concluded that they were just very confident. Their confidence bamboozled us into believing they know what they were talking about. While in the back of their mind, they knew that they had very skilled people to solve the problem. Don't get me wrong every person with SME or Senior in their title aren't putting on a façade. Those people, typically, downplay their title a lot. They know that there is so much more to learn.

Many of my friends have the same attitude about their titles. I have friends with very important jobs: doctors, lawyers, Commanding Officers, 2nd in command at large government organizations. Yet, they all give me the same eye roll when I hype up their position. "It's just a title," they'll say. Then they'll tell me "all I do is..." Which is met more often than not with, "Nuh uh. It's gotta be more to it." They'll say, "Nope. That's it." That's the exact conversation I have with my friend who's the Commanding Officer at her location. I was telling her that we were patching the servers at work. She said, "You know in my mind all you are doing is clicking next, next, next." I responded with, "Yes. That is what I do. They pay me loads of money to press next." As predicted, "Nuh uh!" "Yes, friend, that is literally all...I...do. The expertise is knowing what to do when 'next' doesn't work. But if I'm doing it right nothing will." I spent the next 20 minutes convincing her I was not lying.

Don't get caught up in titles, since they are often arbitrary. Yet another example: I once read a resume where the applicant's last job title was "Team Liaison." Sounds fancy af. After reading the description of what the candidate did, I learned that he sent emails to the team and recorded the minutes during meetings. That's similar to calling a panhandler an entrepreneur. Keep in mind that since job titles mean something different at every employer, your job description means more than your actual title. Therefore, I ask that you don't bypass a job opportunity because the title is intimidating. Don't think someone is more experienced than you simply because Senior is in their title. Sometimes "Senior" just means they've been doing it for a long time and doing something for a long time does not mean you are good at it.

23 confidence

The question of confidence is hugely popular among women, especially women just joining the workforce. How can I gain more confidence? *You're* so confident; how can I be like you? And let me tell you: confidence is natural to some, but it can also be learned. Hell, I learned it. Now, my friends constantly tell me they wish they were as confident as I am, and I immediately give them the "bitch please" face. I don't feel confident, and just because I learned *how* to be doesn't mean I'm like that naturally. When I'm alone at home, I'm mo' confident than a muthafucka. Move over, Trina, 'cause I'm the baddest bitch!

Early in my career, I was the least confident person around. The moment I was presented with a situation in which I needed to radiate confidence, I crawled into a shell. I'd unconsciously make myself submissive to anyone who exuded just a fraction more confidence than me. In fact, the idea of even trying to act more confident didn't come until much later, when I was at lunch with a friend discussing my problem with weight loss. I told him all the work required, and he simply looked at me and said, "Then do it." I immediately was like, it's not that easy. Again, he looked me dead in my optic lens and said, "I didn't say it was going to be easy. I said do it." It was then that I realized the key to confidence. My friend wasn't confident I could lose all the weight (that sounds bad, but ignore!), but he *was* confident that the solution was correct, and he was willing to do what was needed to prove it. I yearned for confidence like that, and even after discovering the key, it took me eight years later in 2013, to finally *decide* to be confident

Before we get into the moment that I oozed confidence, let me set the backstory. There's a guy I met in college, let's call him William, who radiated confidence. To me, he was the person that inspired you to do things and live a better life. When Will spoke, he made it seem like nothing that you attempted was too big. If you failed, no big deal. If you said this to Will directly, he would look at you like you've lost your fucking mind. He is quite humble and nonchalant. Sweet and kind, but somehow still tells it like it is. His best friend, Kyle, is equally as charismatic and magnificent. When the two of them were together, they made you feel like you could conquer the world with the same amount of effort as lifting a straw. Although they were younger than me, I looked up to them. I wanted to exhibit that same confidence. I wanted to have conviction in my statements, like them. To sound as if I already knew what the answer was before I even knew the problem!

Will and I ended up working together as Nuclear Engineers. Shortly after starting my tenure there, I transitioned from Nuclear

Engineer to SharePoint Administrator[79]. On my team, there was an old guy that sat across from me, Jack. Jack had been in this position for thirty damn years. Sitting at the same desk. What I've learned is people his age was very loyal to their companies. Once someone got to their desired rank they would typically stay in that position until retirement.

Merely days away from his retirement, I realized he and I were the same rank. I started pondering if this was my fate. What was my desired career outcome? I didn't want to stay in this position until retirement, but I knew that moving up would be hard to do since most people in that organization stayed in one spot once they hit their desired rank.

During that time, I had a friend who presented me with an offer to move up to D.C. for a new job. At first, I didn't want to. I was happy in my position. According to success in my city, I'd made it. I had a home, car and a stable job. There was no reason to leave. However, there was something in the back of my mind that reminded me that this may be my final destination. Tossing caution to the wind, I interviewed for the position and was made an offer. When I got the call to negotiate my salary, I was presented with a salary that was a damn good salary by Portsmouth standards. Yet I knew I'd have to pay mortgage and rent, and that the cost of living in the D.C. area was double that of Portsmouth. Still, I had nothing to lose! If I didn't get the job, then I already had a job and a stable life in Portsmouth. The worst that could happen is that I would be in the exact same position I was in. Nothing would change.

---

[79] Interestingly, I didn't like anything about being a Nuclear Engineer beside saying I was one, see Titles

When the offer came in, I knew I had to be confident. Three things helped me channel my inner Will and Kyle. I stood tall and channeled Will's mannerisms. It helped it was a phone interview, and they couldn't see me so...there's that. But standing tall helped me get into the right frame of mind. I reminded myself that the worse they can say is 'no.' I told them the offer was acceptable, but I needed more money. I was nervous as hell. I thought the amount of money I was asking for was ludicrous. I wondered who I was to make such demands. They were hesitant. I was told they needed to speak with their higher-ups, and I would get a response in less than twenty-four hours. We ended the call. The moment I hung up the phone, I knew I'd finally found confidence. I couldn't believe that I'd gotten the guts to ask for so much money and they didn't immediately say 'no.' It was literally $35,000 more than what I was currently making. Insane! $35,000 is how much I made as a teacher.[80] I felt a rush of relief and power at having conquered my first attempt. I was jumping for joy even though the offer wasn't even confirmed. I was overjoyed simply because I had the courage to get through the conversation. Now that the conversation was over, I couldn't help but think, "Why was I so scared?" At worst, they would have said 'no' and my life wouldn't have changed.

That was the conversation that led me to truly believe you can gain confidence if you implement this one thing: fake the funk! The saying, "Fake it 'til you make it" is exactly what I'm proposing here. Find

---

[80] Have I mentioned how teachers need to be paid more in this chapter?

your inner Will. Your inner Beyoncé. Your inner Barack. Whoever that person is that you admire their ability to command a room. Channel their mannerisms, their stance, their facial expressions, and whatever else. Regardless of who it is you are channeling, stand tall. It helps to feel dominant. If you can't stand, sit tall. Elongate your back and feel yourself hovering over the people or person you want seeing you exuding confidence. In that moment, you are no longer yourself, but you are Beyoncé.[81] Like Beyoncé, people already know who you are when you walk into the room. All eyes and ears are on you. You already know the answers to the questions they are unable to solve. Be Yoncé![82]

And remember, you only need to be Yoncé for a few moments to get through what you need to get through. Just exude that air for ten minutes for that job interview. Embody Bey for that promotion. Manifest Sasha Fierce to tell off a co-worker.[83] Finding your inner shero (or hero or nonconforming-ero) and embracing it for a few moments to get through the tough moment will help you build your confidence. Each time you do it, you will feel like you are channeling less and less because you find more of your rhythm. Your personal groove. Over time, you'll know what you'll want, and you'll just go for it without a second thought.

Back to my story. When the hiring company gave me a call back, they offered me the job with the higher pay! My technique worked. I was overwhelmed with joy that I jumped up and down and silent screamed in

---

[81] Well, use her for example

[82] See what I did there? I'm proud of that statement and I won't apologize for it.

[83] I have run out of Beyoncé synonyms, so I'll stop here.

the conference room. All the nervous jitters instantly evaporated. I was scared to do something, and I did it anyway. This just solidified my first memorable confidence experience. It helped me to see that I could do something that I was terrified to do, and not spontaneously combust. I didn't melt. I didn't die. I wasn't yelled at. I survived. I landed on my feet. And I'll survive the next time. I was fortunate that it was a positive experience. It gave me the confidence I needed to try the technique again. I like to think of it as the catalyst to a wave of confident moments.

I recognize that if this experience didn't go well the likelihood that I would summon the courage to try it again would have diminished. And if I ever tried again, it would have been a long time later. I find that a lot of women tend to have that mentality. Of course, everyone knows the saying: "If at first you don't succeed, give up. That shit didn't work." Wait. What? That's not how it goes. Although we know the actual saying, for some reason we get all butt hurt when things don't go our way the first time and give up. At times, we predict the conclusion due to past trials, but fail to realize that every situation is totally different. Regardless of what your situation is, there are always new variables. The people are different. The job is different. What you're asking for is different. The time is different. Everything is different, so why should you expect the outcome to be the same? In Mark Manson's book, *The Subtle Art of Not Giving a F*ck*, he states, "You don't know the outcome until you try it." So, go out there and fake that confidence until it becomes a part of who you are.

My sentiment is that you cannot guarantee the outcome of any situation. You must attempt to sway the odds in your favor. Today, there are several ways we can say this, "Shoot your shot," "You gotta be in it to win it," "You miss 100% of the shots you don't take." Take that first step. Conquer that first time. The rush of the first time is like nothing else you'll experience. It gives you a sixth sense. You start to see with 20/20 vision. You are now a clairvoyant. OK, that may be a little extreme. But that's what I felt like after my first attempt. For some reason, I thought it would be harder. Maybe I thought there would be more yelling. But nope. That's all folks! Either they will or they won't. Either he does or he doesn't. Just a simple 'yes' or 'no' is what it comes down to. There aren't too many more options after that. Mustering the courage to try that first time to break the confidence hymen. Just like sex. The first time is the scariest and most awkward. Even if you think you know what's going to happen, you don't. But after that hymen breaks you think, "...is this it?? I mean, ok..." However, the more you do it, the more you learn your rhythm. You know what you want and go for it. It becomes more natural and even though in the beginning you were just mimicking what you've seen, you start to find your own groove. It starts to become a part of who you are.

To conclude, confidence is like sex. You fake it in the beginning (because you don't know what you are doing) and it's scary as hell. Then after practice, it just comes naturally, and you've learned enough tricks that you can teach other people. (This is a strange analogy. Maybe don't use this. Just forget I said anything.)

---

s o r r y • n o t • s o r r y

"Sorry not sorry." I'm not referring to Demi Lovato's 2017 hit single. I'm speaking about how women constantly apologize. We apologize for every damn thing. We apologize for shit we didn't even do! Someone bumps into us, and we say, "Oh, I'm sorry." You didn't do anything! You weren't the problem. You were standing there, and a person crashed into you. Yet, we are conditioned to apologize for something that we didn't do. Apologizing is just a side effect of being taught that we are an inconvenience. When we feel that we are inconveniencing someone or being bothersome, we apologize for it. We are apologizing for taking up space. For existing. This can show as a lack of confidence. We tend to feel grateful to just be in the room, to be amongst certain people, or to even be a part of the conversation. This gratitude coaches us to believe that we shouldn't cause any inconvenience while we are there. So, we'll start of a sentence with, "I'm sorry." We apologize for turmoil that someone else, who has nothing to do with us, inflicted on another person. Karl comes to you and tell you that the spreadsheet is not correct. You didn't create the spreadsheet; you don't even know who Karl is. The first thing we do is try to fix the problem. It's not your problem to fix but you try anyway. Then apologize when you can't fix the problem and Karl is still upset. You tell yourself that you are apologizing for not being able to fix the issue. Yet, this was Karl's issue the whole time! Instead of taking on Karl's problem as your own, you can redirect Karl to the correct resource or guide him to solve his own problem.

Whenever a woman apologizes to me, I ask her why she is apologizing. A lot of the times I don't wait for a response but like to see her mill over what she actually thinks she is apologizing for. Other times, I'll press on to get an actual answer because I want her to see that she has gotten so used to apologizing for everything. I once dropped a box of paper clips and my co-worker said, "Oh, I'm sorry." I laughed and asked what she was sorry for. She proclaimed that she was sorry for the trouble I'm going through. Girl! That is a reach!

I started monitoring when I feel I'm about to apologize when there is no need. If you apologize for everything and anything, even things that are not your fault, over time those apologies mean nothing. I've been training myself to make my apologies mean something, and that means being selective in what I apologize for. Make sure your "I'm sorry's" mean you apologize instead of "Excuse Me" or "Move bitch!"

24

give me my coins

It's common knowledge that females are notoriously paid less than men. According to the 2015 U.S. Census Bureau (most current census report at the time of this writing), women earn 79.8 percent of a man's earnings. I didn't even have to do the math to get that number. There is literally a column on the report that says, "Women's earnings as a percentage of men's earnings." Men's earnings are a fucking standard to measure against! It's insane that it's 2020, and we are still talking about equality.

While I'm always down for equal pay and believe that a substantial portion of the blame for this imbalance falls on society, I'm here to argue that some of the blame falls on us women. We are a part of the "society" that is perpetuating this antiquated narrative. We are so upset when we see the skewed numbers that we don't take a step back to look at the situation objectively. If we are truly honest with ourselves, we will recognize that we often claim to be the victim. Once we've deemed ourselves the victim, we are relinquished from all fault. We are then allowed to blame someone else. We don't have to push ourselves to do more or to step outside our comfort zones. Our comfort zones allow for excuses and drown out any resolve.

I have learned there are a myriad of reasons why women don't ask for their worth: too polite, too afraid, don't want to have an awkward conversation, or want to avoid conflict, to name a few. At some point in our career, we've experienced one (or all of these) concerns. If you're just stepping into the workplace after college, chances are you'll come across these sooner rather than later. Women who are well-established in their careers struggle with asking for their worth, and it's even worse for those that are just beginning. Let's dive into how I came to realize my own worth and how you can too.

Let's refer back to my story about confidence. I was under the impression that I would somehow upset this person that I've never even met if I asked for the amount I wanted. I didn't want some company I wasn't attached to to "not like me." How insane! Women are trained to please people more than our male counterparts. Society teaches girls that they must be polite. That they must avoid upsetting someone else. This hinders us when we have to speak up for ourselves because we are now afraid to disrupt the environment and ask for what is due. We are constantly concerning ourselves with the other person's perspective that we perpetually neglect our own. This continues the vicious cycle of a society of unconfident women.

We tend to feel that asking for a comparable salary would be impolite or an imposition. We shy away from asking for what we really want. Some of that shyness comes from fear. But fear of what? The answer: rejection. We don't want to be rejected. When it comes to occupational resilience, guys can bounce back quicker than women. Guys are more willing to force themselves through a situation until they get results. They will go through trial and error far longer than a woman. Women will stop shortly after a few failed attempts. Men have the audacity to attempt. They attempt to get away with what we believe is impossible, while they have been groomed to think, "...but what if it works." Women, on the other hand, think, "What if it *doesn't* work?" Men slowly learn to shoot for the stars and brush off any rejection.

I'm not saying that rejection doesn't hurt men, nor am I trying to say women don't handle rejection well. I'm proposing that men are able to bounce back quicker because they have more practice with rejection than we have. Unconsciously (or consciously), we've played it safe. We've lowballed ourselves because we are afraid that the number, we want may be too high. We'll say a number that we know will not be rejected. We are just grateful for the opportunity to be hired. We work harder than all the men to prove we are more competent, while secretly fuming because we are getting 80 percent of the pay. but doing 120 percent of the work.

It wasn't until I was a mid-level employee when I was first aware of high-paid mediocrity. A new employee asked me to help him register for company benefits online. This particular website automatically showed your salary in plain text in the navigation pane. While waiting for him to add his information in, I accidentally glanced over and saw he was making $30,000 more than me. Since he was an older gentleman, I assumed he was an expert in his field.[84] I took note of the salary and decided that it would be my new goal.

As time went on, I learned more about this guy. He is Kevin from the chapter A Minority Female Engineer. If you didn't read that yet, Kevin was the dick that didn't want to ask for my help, and then blamed me for missing his deadline. In the time that I worked alongside Kevin, I don't ever recall him producing a deliverable to the customer. A deliverable is basically evidence that you've been doing something; it's the end result. Kevin never completed anything. He would complain until he was shifted to another project, and just jumped around working solo until they let him go.

Against my will, I learned more from Kevin than I expected. Kevin showed me that mediocrity pays *well*! I started thinking, if Kevin's fucking mediocrity gets $30,000 more than me, then I should be getting $50,000; at least I know what the fuck I'm doing! From that moment on, I decided that I would work towards that number. Knowing that I was vastly more knowledgeable and skillful than many of my cohorts gave me the confidence to go for my worth.

---

[84] See Titles; for truths I learned.

the • motto

My first job was at a Wendy's restaurant making $5.15/hr. (Ancient times!) I was there for about a year before I got a raise of ten cents. That's right, ladies and gentlemen, I was making a cool $5.25 per hour after working for one whole year! I stayed there until I went to college. The scholarship program I was in didn't allow any activities or jobs your freshman year so you could focus entirely on your studies.

Summer after my freshman year, I got a new job at Lowe's Home Improvement. Nervously, I asked for six dollars per hour, and these suckers went for it! Ha! Ha! (What a show of the times!?) I stayed there for about six months. I attempted to work and go to school. However, I noticed that my grades started to suffer, so I had to quit. The summer after my sophomore year, I went back to Wendy's at $7.00 per hour. (Look at me now!)

This trend started a practice I still implement; always ask for more, whether it's a dollar or $10,000. I always wanted to make sure that I was always progressing financially. For a while, I lived by the motto, "Make more than the last position." This held strong until I ran into a few situations that forced me to get rid of my blanket statement and make a few exceptions.

Exception #1

You can accept less if the job is something that will make you happy (happiness >> money).

<u>Exception #2</u>

You can accept less if you will gain a skill that will earn you more money in the long run.

I made these modifications to ensure that I didn't sacrifice happiness or skills for money. Apart from these exceptions, however, I always either accept the same amount, or go for higher. Never less.

Around my second real job, I arbitrarily decided that I was going to have a numerical salary goal. Once again, I said, "Self...by forty, you will be making one million dollars." Okay, maybe it wasn't a million, but at the time it seemed like an insane number. I'm from a small town, and when I was a public-school teacher making $45,000 a year, I was making more than any member of my family. For me, that number I set may as well have been one million. It was certainly double what I was making which sounded ridiculous, but still a reachable goal.

After about a year of making this very random declaration, I started to figure out my strategy to get to the designated salary goal. During my research I discovered that in order to reach the goal, I would have to move. Moving away from a city that I was born and raised in for thirty years was a very difficult decision to make. Most of my family still resides there. There were only a handful of family members who moved away. As the saying goes,

To get something you've never had, you must do something you've never done.

The city I lived in had very few opportunities to make that amount. Additionally, those opportunities were very senior-level positions that would take me years to work up to. I had an arbitrary goal to hit. If I'd lived in a more metropolitan area, moving wouldn't have been something that I'd have to sacrifice. In a more robust area, you can find your niche pretty much anywhere. There's a greater selection of areas from technology to art in a more densely populated area.

Yet, here I was faced with the decision to leave home in order to hit my target. When I left, I honestly didn't know how I was going to manage to get to that salary. However, I managed to hit my target within three months of moving! I recognize that that's insane. I managed to double the salary I was making in February by May! This led me to two things: my goal was obviously too small for the area I was in and I needed a new "unreachable" goal. Being better acclimated with the new way of life, I understood how to better architect a goal. This goal was half my salary. This goal helped me plan my career path. Again, I had to figure out what steps I needed to take to reach said goal. But how was I going to take those steps if I didn't know my own worth?

In my journey, I've learned that with experience comes a level of salary confidence! Recall my phone call where I feigned confidence[85]; I modelled that behavior for about three more years. The salary confidence seemed like it just happened suddenly, but it was a gradual progression.

---

[85] See Confidence

Imagine a headhunter sending you an email with a job description that has piqued your interest. You reach out with:

I am interested in this position. Please send over the salary range and benefit package.

Send. That's it.

Wait, what?! You didn't thank them for this opportunity. You didn't give them your resume. You didn't do research on the company. Yup! At this level, you know your worth. You've held interviews. You know how this goes. You know that they need you, otherwise they wouldn't have sought you out. These simple sentences demonstrate that you are frequently sought after, and your deciding factor will be the salary. You don't want to waste your time nor theirs with a dog and pony show.

Your first thought is probably that's unprofessional. Go back and read it. What part is unprofessional? I *said* "please." The real word that you are looking for is impolite. It is also not impolite. It's just direct. It lets them know that I am interested in the position, but I want to know how much it's willing to pay before we discuss anything further. Knowing your worth helps to get you to this point.

Knowing your worth isn't always the easiest thing to determine, especially as a woman. We are notorious for underbidding ourselves. I found that if I could just have a reference, determining my worth would be so much easier. And that's the difficult part. You can go online, but usually they give you a national average. The national average doesn't really help because they include major cities like San Francisco and New York City, where the cost of living is much higher. That means $100,000 there may be on the low end of the pay scale, but $100,000 in Huntsville, Alabama, is on the high end. Sometimes you'll find a job that's close to your position description. Now you must guess what you should be making. What would *definitely* help is if you can just know what the other people in your company are getting paid for the same position. However, in most companies, there is a clause that states you can't discuss your salary with other employees. This is typically added to allow for negotiation. The company saves money when they are able to pay variable costs per employee. To help resolve this issue, someone created an app called Blind—Anonymous Professional Network. Its goal is to help individuals get a leg up on interviews, salaries, and the workplace without revealing their identity.

I lucked up because in the beginning of my career, I was hired as a government employee and I had the pleasure of working with a few contractors that were very open about finances.[86] One of the guys, José, was very open and shared his salary with me. I learned he was making $20,000 more than me! Instantly, I was jealous. I managed my green monster by rationalizing how there wasn't really much I could do to increase my salary. Since I was in the government, getting promoted to a supervisor or having sheer longevity were my only options. There were limited supervisory positions which people held until their retirement.

---

[86] Who later became my financial mentors; See Dots and Circles

The first time I negotiated my salary was for a position outside of the government, so it was helpful to know my co-worker's salary as a baseline. Additionally, I considered the cost of living, and my current and new expenses. I asked for a number that I felt was on the high scale. I was hired making $30,000 more. Winning!

Oh, so I thought. A few weeks after I started, I learned I was the only one not making six figures. I was immediately furious. The guy that revealed he was making six figures even admitted he knew less than I did. I vowed that for my next position, I'd negotiate for six figures. I couldn't help but giggle when I got the opportunity to ask; for me, these were whimsical numbers. The moment I saw an offer letter with six digits on it, I knew I was living a dream. I'd officially made more money than both my parents combined!

Every career move after that, each new number seemed insane more than the last. But I started to recognize my worth, so asking for more began to get easier. Don't get me wrong, I'm still flummoxed by the amount of money people are willing to pay me. I attribute this to two things: coming from a small town where $45,000 was a lot of money and being a woman afraid to ask for what she's worth. Luckily, I was able to overcome that part.

I live by the commonly used Black proverb, "You have to work twice as hard to get half as much." For me, a Black female, I have to work four times as hard to get half as much. I have to prove that just because I'm a woman doesn't mean I'm a ditz, and just because I'm Black doesn't mean I'm lazy. Since I'm over here working so damn hard, I want my coins!

25

all my coins

There are many stories where Sally tried to get a promotion and failed?

What's the point of you trying if she couldn't get it, am I right?

We tend to base our truths off the experience of others. While sometimes this can be helpful, the truth is you don't really know Sally's situation. Sally could have been trash. She could be the world's worst employee asking for a promotion. Yet things like this discourage us from pursuing a raise. We tend to blame the lack of upward movement to the wage gap, not realizing that our fear of asking for what we deserve perpetuates the gap. We'll blame it on sexism before giving anyone the opportunity to reject us.

Why are we afraid to ask for more? Instead, we just sit at our desks and complain. Instead of complaining, let's try to ask for what we want. You won't know until you try. Let's stop assuming that we know how things will turn out. The truth is we don't know. As I mentioned before, everything about this opportunity is different. Different time, different people, different circumstances. You can't possibly know what the outcome will be. You can assume but you don't know unless you shoot your shot.

Now I just want to put a disclaimer out there because inevitably there will be someone that will deduce something that I am not implying. I am not implying that the lack of trying is the sole reason for the wage gap. I'm not implying that sexism doesn't play a role. I believe that women are shorted even if we are the biggest boss with all the sauce. What I'm hoping to convey is there are other factors that contribute to the wage discrepancies that we can, and should, take accountability for. We need to look within ourselves to make sure that we aren't constantly blaming external sources when we've made no effort to resolve the issue ourselves.

Remember that project I was on with Kevin? Well, during that same time, Steve[87], the business analyst, left the company. He had started the project the same time I did. Steve had overseen talking to the customer and finding out what they wanted so that I could develop it. When Steve left, the customer was more comfortable discussing things with me since I had the same historical knowledge of the project as Steve. Therefore, it was left on me to do his job as well as mine since I was also the Senior Developer on the project. I was expected to do my and Steve's job until they hired someone. My company told me they were hiring

---

[87] Dude everyone has a fake name, you should know that by now.

someone to replace Steve; just give them three weeks. Four months later, Steve wasn't replaced, and the customer didn't want to deal with anyone but me. This is when the age-old adage came to mind: "In order to get something, you've never had you must do something you've never done." In this case, it was recognizing my worth. I'd never been responsible for so much on a project. That's when I recognized that I have *leverage*. The project's history and future laid with me. If I were to leave, no one else would know as much about the project, and It would likely go under. This was more of a management issue than anything else. Their mismanagement was my opportunity. I had the leverage to ask for damn near anything I wanted.

The only question now was what did I want? More. More what? ... **looks around**...just more. This was my flaw at the time. I didn't know exactly what I wanted, so they could have given me anything, and I would have been happy as long as it was more than what I currently had. They could have given me a kitten and I would have been happy, simply because it was something that I didn't have. I just knew I deserved more. I just didn't know what that meant exactly. I hadn't put a value on my worth. But I decided to go for it anyway.

One day in October, I gathered my confidence and walked in my program manager's office and asked to be compensated for the extra work that I'd been doing. He said, "Oh! Yes! Yes! OK, I'll tell Karen. She deals with this kinda stuff." I'm like, "Oh cool! That was way easier than I expected." Karen was the other program manager. From what I understood, she dealt more with the business side of things, where my direct program manager worked daily on the project.

When Karen called me into her office about a week later, I didn't think too much of it. I just thought I'd have to fill out some paperwork. I sat down across from Karen and she asked, "Why do you think you deserved to be compensated?" I was immediately taken aback. Mainly because I thought I had this in the bag! I didn't think any explanation was needed. My work spoke for itself. I relaxed a little and just thought, "Tim didn't get her up to speed. Men!" I nonchalantly explained that I was doing both my work and Steve's, so I needed to be handed my coins. She still didn't seem to be convinced and said, "And that's why you want a raise?" I began to get flustered. What was happening? In my mind, there was absolutely no question that I deserved a raise! Why didn't she see that? I started to feel attacked. I straightened up. I explained how I hadn't taken a day off in several months, and when I finally did take two consecutive days off, I was called at home and informed that my presence was required in the office. I itemized all the things that I did on a regular basis and the extra hours I put in. I also took this opportunity to inform her that I was actively looking for another position (even though I wasn't). She seemed unphased by my comments. She just looked at me pointedly and said, "Ok. Thank you for stopping by." And that was the end of the conversation.

After that conversation, I grew extra salty about my meeting with my program managers. So much so that I really *did* start looking for another job. I didn't hear anything else from her or the other manager until Christmas. In my final check of the year, I received a 5 percent raise and a sizable bonus! The gesture showed me that I was valuable. It helped me recognize my worth. Granted, they were pretty unprofessional for not communicating their intentions. But also, I think they called my bluff when I was still there two months after my notification of looking for new employment.

Now, I know this seems like I seized the first opportunity that came to me and just ran with it, but that wasn't the case. For me to get to that moment, a few things had to be acknowledged. First, I had to recognize that I was worthy of more. How does one measure that? Easy. What did they originally hire you to do? Are you still doing those things? Are you doing additional things? Doing something completely different? Do you feel overworked and underpaid? If you answered yes to any of those last three questions, then you are worth more. You deserve a raise. In the technical world, this is called *scope creeping*. They ask you to take care of small things here and there. You don't mind because it's small. Then they see that you are a worker that can get things done. So, they start assigning you work Karl should be doing because he's incompetent. Now you are being stretched thin, and all because you happen to be competent. This is the way I see it. If you are doing Karl's work, then you need to be getting Karl's check too! Work creeping notoriously happens to women because we are nurturing, helpful people. We do things to help or streamline a situation, and often don't recognize the scope creeping is even happening. The next thing you know, you are performing a new function. While I like to call that a resume builder, I also like to call my manager and ask for more money!

Second, I had to recognize that my company wasn't going to voluntarily give me my well-deserved coins. Obviously, I don't know everyone's company and industry, so I speak generally when I say you are just a series of numbers to your employer. Basically, you are employee #007 earning X amount of dollars. You are an entry in a spreadsheet, and while your manager may care about you, the company cares only about its profits. That's why so many of them like to appease their employees by giving them things that are economical, like awards and certificates. Oh, you want to be recognized for your hard work? Here's a piece of paper that says, "You are the best," and $100 gift card to Applebee's. Happy? Yeah. Ok, now keep bringing in thousands for the company! For many companies, giving a certificate and a gift card is cheaper than giving you a 2 percent raise. It accomplishes the same thing: soothing your desire to be recognized. Their way, however, saves them money when going about your way would cost them money.

In my opinion, awards and certificates should be for doing a great job at what I was hired to do. If you pay me to make milkshakes and I help with the lunch rush, then make the gift cards rain! However, if I developed a process to efficiently manage the lunch rush every time, then "Give me my coins!" Just remember that more often not, you will work in a company like the ones I described, and when you're looking for that raise, you will have to ask for what you want. That's what I did.

The last thing I had to recognize was my leverage. When asking for a promotion or raise, you have to be aware of the cards you hold. To date, I have asked for a raise three times. In the first instance, I knew that my leverage was holding the majority of the project knowledge, being the subject matter expert on the software, and having a relationship with the client where they preferred me. Additionally, I knew timing was everything. Being conscious of when you ask is extremely important. Those four factors put me in a position where I could ask for a raise, and I was armed with my leverage when I walked in Karen's office.

The second time I asked for a raise, I was aware that the position I was in required a solid six to eight months to get access to all the systems, plus another six months to get up to speed. Not only was it difficult for someone to get ramped up on all the systems, it was just hard to find someone with all the qualifications required for the position. While I knew I wasn't the strongest person on the team, the company couldn't afford to lose *any* member of the team. Our project manager secretly lived in fear that we would finally get fed up and quit. With this in mind, I easily was able to get a bump in salary.

The third time I'd only been on the job for six months before I asked. My leverage was very similar to the first time where I had the historical knowledge and if I left, they would be in a bad position. I was really taking a chance asking six months in, and I wouldn't usually recommend doing it. I typically like to establish my worth over the course of a year, but in this situation, my value was established within three months. I was nervous about asking so soon, but I knew that I had leverage, and I wanted to pounce on the opportunity.

Another important factor in asking for a raise is timing. Recently, I was encouraging a friend to ask for a promotion. The next time I saw them, I asked if they asked for the promotion yet. They said, "No. There is a lot going on right now. I'm going to wait for it to die down a bit. Everyone is stressed over this project we are working on." It took all of me not to scream in my friend's face! That is the time to strike!

Like the stock market, the best time to buy is when shit has hit the fan.[88] The best time to ask for a raise is when things are shitty. Not the "we are letting people go" shitty, but more like "Deadlines! DEADLINES! DEADLINES!!" shitty. When they have so much work and you are a key player in the game, that's when you ask. When the project is on the cusp of some pinnacle point, you ask. It reminds them of your value. It forces them to see what they would lose if you were to leave, so make sure you asked yourself those three questions to determine if you're worth more beforehand.

For those reading, you probably think that I'm talking as if it's all easy peasy lemon squeezy to get a raise. This is a falsehood! There is so much mental preparation that goes into asking for a raise, even more so than just determining your worth, leverage, and voice. You also must prepare yourself for the very real possibility of the following three outcomes: you are replaced, you don't get anything you want, or you may have to compromise.

Each time I decided that I was going to ask for a raise, I had to have a solution for each scenario. What if they fire me? What if they say

---

[88] See Stocks to understand this reference

no? What if they don't give me *all* the coins? What is my plan? What am I going to do? Do I have a job offer already? If so, am I willing to actually take the job? If not, am I willing to face turning it down, but still working somewhere they didn't want to give me a raise? If they aren't going to give me the full amount, what is the minimum I'm willing to take? These are all actual questions I ask myself each time I prepare to ask for a promotion.

While leverage is important, having a strategy is even more important. Remember my story at the beginning; I didn't know what I wanted. I didn't have any real rebuttal when it came to fight for why I wanted more. I approach every raise request with the assumption they will not just say, "Ok. Cool beans." I like to have a fallback plan, and typically it's an offer from another company. This shows my company that someone else thinks I'm worth a certain amount, and that they should too. This definitely helps with the fight. Go into the conversation knowing what you are willing to accept as the bare minimum. Consider this: You ask for a $10,000 raise, and they offer you a $5,000 increase and $5,000 in bonuses. Are you ok with that? Some may think, "Same thing." Actually, it's not the same. A $10,000 raise means that next year your salary will be $10,000 more. With the $5,000 raise and $5000 bonus, next year your salary will only increase by $5,000. Additionally, you are taxed higher on the $5,000 bonus. Overall, getting the latter will result in less money than the $10,000 salary increase. Give me *all* my coins, sir!

Another situation to consider is approaching your employer with a legit job opportunity, and they counter the offer. This is quite flattering.

Essentially what they are saying is, we can't lose you. At this point, you need to figure out what it is that you really want. Do you just want more money? Do you want a change of scene? Do you want to learn something new? Be prepared to know what you want before you go into these conversations. Be able to articulate what it is that you are looking for. They may be able to accommodate you.

Once I was offered a position that offered me $20,000 less than what I was currently making, but I would be changing to a new career field. I would be coming in at a junior level, so it made sense that I was getting a chop in my salary. However, due to the field, I knew that I would be able to return to my current pay with a little experience. When I approached my employer, they countered with $20,000 **more** than my current salary and first dibs on projects! As enticing as the offer was, I knew that I wouldn't be happy staying there. and what I really wanted was the new opportunity. I had to go into the meeting with my program manager knowing that nothing could keep me there.

Being aware of your worth and not being afraid to let others know that you know you're worthy will aid you in your path to a pay increase. Through performance reviews, you should know if you are doing a good job. During your performance reviews, if you consistently hear that you're doing a stellar job, then this can be that reassurance you need to ask for what you want. It doesn't necessarily have to be money; you could ask for more time, a different project, or training. I like to tell women there are only two reasons your employer is reluctant to give you a raise: your performance or lack of funds. If they really want you, they will make a way.

26

outro

"Success is a journey, not a destination. The doing is often more important than the outcome." - Arthur Ashe

Life is hard. Truer words have never been spoken. Those three simple words can carry so much weight. Sometimes, the things that we think are hard are actually simple, but then life throws a curve ball at us and gives us questions you can't necessarily find in a book. Such as, how do you be a parent to your parents? What do you do if your friend chips your tooth? When you move to a new state, where do you learn about the new state laws? There are just so many things that you have to learn through trial and error. Luckily, we live in the age of information, so you aren't always completely lost on any topic. There are blogs and videos on the most obscure things. Once, I didn't know how to open a tube of caulk so I YouTube'd it. Thank goodness someone thought, there's probably some idiot out there that doesn't know how to do this and made a video.

We all wish there was a guide that we could just open and it explains how we get through this part of life. It's even harder for those that aren't surrounded by people that are successful enough to help them. The struggle is real. We all want fruitful lives and the end goal is to be happy. Something I learned along the way is that being rich doesn't equal happiness (it sure as hell helps though). We just want to be able to wake up and enjoy where we are and what we do. Some people feel like they are a victim of their circumstances and will just give in to that. Then there are people like you who will think,

"Shit, now what?"

acknowledgements

My family should come first, right? OK. Thanks, y'all for putting up with me. I know I'm not easy and that I can make life difficult. I sometimes I'm *too* logical about things. I appreciate you loving me despite that. I hope that I continue to live up to be the best auntie to The Boy, The Girl, The Little Girl and The Baby, also known as Keonté, Shonté, Jazmin, and Eli'Jah. To my sister-in-law, Ichesia, who I love for not only how incredible she is but also for making our family better. To John, for giving me a chance to prove you right. My little baby sister, De'Elsie, whose perseverance knows no bounds. To my big brother, Donté, I literally wouldn't be able to survive without you. To Carmazine Lindell Wright Veal Sharpe. (I mean, how could I not put the full government?) You gave me every tool you had to prepared me for a world that wasn't prepared for me! To my dad, who never doubted I would be ok.

Thanks to every aunt, uncle, and cousin. Thanks all the friends that encouraged, supported, and helped me along the way: Krystal, Sherelle, Renee, Latisha, Lauren, Edward, Ayisha, Stephanie, Frederick,

Lisa, Brittni, Jeremy, Samelia, Ebony, Jessica A., all my line sisters, all the ΔΣΘ ΕΘ #14, my hunnie bunnie, and anyone else I forgot.

Also, special thanks to my editor, Felice Laverne of Art + Deco Agency.

Erica Veal age: 5   grade: Kindergarden
received this on June 3, 1988
Her teacher was name Mrs. Robinson
The school was Douglas Park Elem.

This was written by
Barry Veal while waiting
to go to work at Vernois Co
of June 6 at 5:22 AM.
with the loving thought
of his family on his mind.

To my little girl Erica who
one day will be able to
read. Then she will find
that I love her with all
my body and mind. I
see in you at this young age
of 5 the possibility of becoming
some one great; the way you
carry around with you paper
and pencil and you always
writing. I hope you will
never stop that eagerness of
wanting to learn because
some day it will all pay off
Loving you Erica, and
your brother Donté always

your Father